Connecting Times
The Sixties in Afro-American Fiction

Connecting Times

The Sixties in
Afro-American Fiction

By
Norman Harris

UNIVERSITY PRESS OF MISSISSIPPI
Jackson and London

MANUFACTURED IN THE UNITED STATES OF AMERICA

91   90   89   88   4   3   2   1

The paper in this book meets the guidelines for permanence and durability of the Committee on Production Guidelines for Book Longevity of the Council on Library Resources.

Library of Congress Cataloging-in-Publication Data

Harris, Norman, 1951-
    Connecting times : the sixties in Afro-American fiction / Norman Harris.
        p.   cm.
    Bibliography: p.
    Includes index.
    ISBN 0-87805-335-2 (alk. paper)
    1. American fiction—Afro-American authors—History and criticism.
2. American fiction—20th century—History and criticism.   3. Afro-Americans in literature.   4. Vietnamese Conflict, 1961-1975—Literature and the war.   5. Civil rights workers in literature.
6. Black power in literature.   I. Title.
PS153.N5H27   1988   87-27685
813'.54'09352039—dc19   CIP

Contents

For my daughter,
Amina Aneesah Harris

Connecting Times
The Sixties in Afro-American Fiction

Introduction:

The Quest for Freedom and Literacy

The war in Vietnam, the civil rights movement, and the black power movement are key events that define the period from 1960 to 1973. The beginning date for the era I designate as the "sixties" is chosen simply because the decade began in 1960. I chose to end the era in 1973 because the war in Vietnam formally ended that year. Additionally, the reelection of President Richard Nixon in 1972 over his liberal opponent, George McGovern, affirmed a shift from the liberalism of the sixties to a new conservatism. Although Watergate was Nixon's undoing, the liberalism associated with the sixties continued to decline. In the thirteen-year period 1960–73 many of America's promises of equality were tested by the three events that structure this study—black involvement in Vietnam, the civil rights movement, and the black power movement.

My interest in this period is in discovering and analyzing how Afro-Americans who were involved in Vietnam or the civil rights or black power movements made sense of their lives or failed to do so when the goals they struggled for were not achieved. This analysis looks at the movement from historical illiteracy to historical literacy, the achievement of which is obtained when individuals find precedents in African or Afro-American history that can help them resolve problems without distorting their personalities. Additionally, this study looks at the strategies individuals used to adjust their lives after the failure of their dreams.

Rather than using primarily sociological sources to accomplish this goal, I use black creative literature in which plot and characterization are structured by the civil rights and black power movements and by black involvement in Vietnam. The novels I analyze that use black involvement in Vietnam to shape plot and characterization are *Captain Blackman* (1972) by John A. Williams, *Coming Home* (1971) by George Davis, and *Tragic Magic* (1978) by Wesley Brown. The novels I analyze that serve the same purpose for the civil rights and black power movements are *Meridian* (1976) by Alice Walker, *Look What They Done to My Song* (1974) by John McCluskey, *The Cotillion or One Good Bull Is Half the Herd* (1971) by John Killens, and *The Last Days of Louisiana Red* (1974) by Ishmael Reed. The creative exploration by these authors of the civil rights and black power movements and black involvement in Vietnam captures the depth and subtlety of a people trying to create and enforce their definitions of themselves and of the world.

In organizing the book in this fashion I am claiming a sociological and explanatory truth in Afro-American literature which can provide a clear basis for understanding the subtleties in motivation and action of Afro-Americans during periods of historically conscious attempts at racial definition. Although social science scholarship might be useful in providing contextual information about the sixties, the creative literature is the basis for this historical analysis. Combining fiction and social science research dealing with the three events on which this study focuses, helps capture the depth and subtlety of actions of a people in the process of self-definition but does not definitively document the era.

Using literature to clarify the social history of the sixties is an acknowledgment of the holistic ways in which Afro-Americans have traditionally perceived the world. This holism has been variously described as "soul," "spirit," "blackness," or "racial consciousness." Each description alludes to an essence whose reality is seen behind or within the creative activities, artifacts, actions, and lifestyles of Afro-Americans. The existence of an Afro-American essence, which influences and helps shape Afro-American life, is well documented in a range of anthropological, historical, linguistic, and psychological texts by writers as diverse as Melville Herskovits, Zora Neale Hurston, John Gwaltney, Laurence Levine, John Blassingame, Geneva Smitherman, Ivory Toldson, and Alfred Pasteur. Despite differences in intellectual content, each writer recognizes that Afro-American life is influenced by forces that cannot be completely explained by reference to empirical data. The total effect of the work of these and other scholars is to verify the existence of an Afro-American culture with its own preoccupations, prejudices, and styles.

In Afro-American literary history, the black aesthetic criticism[1] of the sixties, which was associated with the black arts and black power movements, was based on an Afro-American essence. Stephen Henderson's *Understanding the New Black Poetry* is perhaps the clearest application of this critical method. Henderson's work is central in two ways to the analysis I wish to make. His criticism is conceptualized and practiced in the context of the ongoing cultural contradiction of double-consciousness, what DuBois labels as a feeling of twoness, of being both African and American. In particular, he notes that the "folk" and the "formal" were and continue to be competing forces in Afro-American creative life and Afro-American life generally. The "folk" refers to the African half of double-consciousness and the "formal" to its American half. Henderson describes the relationship between the two as "perhaps too subtle to be called dialectic." He concludes this part of his argument by noting that the folk has had the most significant influence on the formal during periods of the "greatest power and originality" (Henderson, 67).

Folk culture exerts the same positive influence upon formal culture as on a fictional character's ability to resolve conflict: the more "immersed"[2] a character is in the folk culture the more likely he/she is to be able to resolve conflicts. This is a central part of my argument, and it will be developed more fully in the chapters that follow. Here I need to return to Henderson's method to make my final point. His concept of saturation, which he defines as "fidelity to the observed or intuited truth of the black experience" (Henderson, 62), simultaneously reinforces the concept of a black essence and leads to a connection between Henderson's critical Method and that of a more recent critic, Robert Stepto.

Stepto's refinement of Northrop Frye's notion of a pregeneric quest myth is important to my study. Frye asserts that quest myths permeate the culture of all people in such fundamental ways that they precede any consideration of literary form. This theory suggests that a culture is directed by certain desires or quests that operate in all spheres of life, not just in areas of artistic endeavor. Stepto asserts that the Afro-American myth is the quest for freedom and literacy. Stepto defines freedom as an end to slavery and literacy as the ability to read and write as well as the ability to read "cultural signs." This second usage is symbolic and is labeled "tribal," indicating that Afro-American cultural symbols have a collective meaning to those members of the "tribe" who are attuned to the culture, who are literate (Stepto, 173–74). Stepto's meaning of tribal literacy and Henderson's concept of saturation both assume the existence of an Afro-American cultural essence evidenced by literary choices, symbolic actions, and any number of other cultural activities.

Stepto's concept of tribal literacy is the basis for an extrapolation I will make, for it returns the quest for freedom and literacy to a philosophical position that asserts the existence of a racial memory, a collective unconsciousness, which some linguists refer to as "deep structure" continuities. Because I have the dual purpose of using literature to understand the social history of the sixties and of not reducing literature to a brand of sociology, I have broadened the definitions of freedom and literacy. I define freedom as knowledge of the various options available in the reservoir of African and Afro-American history; freedom is thus knowledge of the racial memory. I define literacy as the application of the racial memory as dictated by the confluence between personality and situation. It is important to emphasize the personal dimension in this definition so as to avoid being prescriptive. Attaching the idea of a black essence to a series of specific activities calcifies the essence and can lead to an ahistorical romanticism. Certainly this was one of the major criticisms of cultural nationalists during the sixties.[3] Again, I use Stepto's work to connect freedom and literacy to a philosophical position that asserts the existence of a collective unconsciousness or racial memory among Afro-Americans.

I believe that the desire to achieve freedom and literacy is a motivating factor in the lives of Afro-Americans and is therefore operative in the creative culture of Afro-America. In the world, the quest for freedom and literacy interacts with existing forms—the workplace, higher education, or any other area—in an effort to redefine those forms to achieve freedom and literacy. This interaction has been ongoing as long as Africans have been in America. A recent example of its operation is the frequent convening by black professionals of workshops and seminars on "networking" in an attempt to discover how to adjust to corporate life. *Black Life in Corporate America: Swimming in The Mainstream* by George Davis and Glegg Wilson is the most sustained treatment of this issue, illustrating, more through what can be deduced from descriptions than from what is asserted, that as black women and men break contact with their culture, their ability to handle the pressures in their professional lives is diminished. Without racial memory (freedom) and the ability to apply it (literacy), such individuals seem condemned to material success and varying levels of self-alienation.

At the other end of the spectrum, the underclass in the black community is admonished by black leaders to seek solutions to problems by reconnecting to Afro-American culture. The black church, black businesses, and the black family are suggested as institutions that can help resolve problems and conflicts. Black leaders and organizations that stress this posture of self-reliance include Jesse Jackson, Richard Hatcher, Operation PUSH, the Urban League, the Black Economic Agenda, and the National Urban Coalition.

The relationship between racial memory and the ability to apply it in a fashion consistent with personality is emphasized by the current generation of black leaders. This is not to suggest that the current trend represents a marked departure from previous attempts at racial development; rather, it is to identify a similarity between the literary influence the folk culture exerts on formal culture during periods of the "greatest power and originality" and its influence on political decisions intended to empower Afro-Americans during periods of racial crisis. As the racial memory is applied through literacy, the forms and methods of Afro-American political change become increasingly creative; Jesse Jackson's Rainbow Coalition is a contemporary example of this point. The quest for freedom and literacy can be used in several ways to explain Afro-American political development; I will limit my use of this concept to analyzing the influences that black involvement in Vietnam and the civil rights and black power movements had on Afro-Americans by studying Afro-American novels in which characterization and plot are shaped by these three historical events.

The quest for freedom and literacy in Afro-American literature interacts with existing forms or genres in much the same way that it interacts with received methods of social change. In particular, it recasts existing forms to meet its needs. Stepto, Henry Louis Gates, Jr., Houston Baker, Jr., and others have discussed the interaction of Afro-American literature and literary criticism with Euro-American forms and modes of criticism, attempting to find similarities, differences, and extensions. Their discussions have used a different framework than the one I am presenting; they acknowledge pregeneric considerations which the Afro-American author brings either to the creative work or to the work of criticism. Borrowing from and recasting Stepto's observations, my argument is that the pregeneric consideration is the quest for freedom and literacy as defined here.

Freedom and literacy interact with the plots of the novels studied in this book to demonstrate the centrality of historical understanding to conflict resolution. Thus the plots of the works chosen for examination are relatively straightforward, even when, as in Reed's work, point of view complicates the plot. Essentially, the novels involve a series of actions and events that move from the dark to the light, from ignorance to clarity, whether or not the conflicts the plots contain are ultimately resolved. In advancing the quest for freedom and literacy, the plots are structured toward racial development, that is, showing a relationship between self-reliance and problem resolution.

Freedom interacts with character development in much the same way it does with plot. Events are structured to provide occasions for characters to improve themselves. The interaction of literacy with character development is necessary to understand the degree to which characters are able to resolve conflicts. For the fictive Afro-Americans fighting in Vietnam, the ability to mollify the conflict of fighting for a country that does not accord them full democratic rights is achieved through historical study and reflection. Although such study does not always result in altering power relationships between blacks and whites, it is certainly necessary for that possibility to exist. Those fictive Afro-Americans affected by Vietnam who do not engage in historical study and reflection are overwhelmed by the war, for they lack anchors. In the civil rights and black power novels a similar connection obtains; those characters who find meaning in the black church, black spirituality, or black music manage to handle the disappointments, resulting from their involvement in these movements. In this fiction, when historical knowledge interacts with a character's personality in a fashion that does not distort that personality, it is usually an indication that the character has obtained literacy.

As noted earlier, the quest for freedom and literacy is also a basis for understanding activism among Afro-Americans in the sixties. Indeed, the shift from the intergrationism associated with the civil rights movement and the early phases of black involvement in Vietnam to the nationalism of the black power movement and of the late phases of black involvement in Vietnam might well be viewed as an elaborate plot, a series of events structured toward achieving a particular emotional impact. That impact, I would argue, is the demonstration that Afro-American culture must be the basis for projecting a future (freedom) and for conflict resolution (literacy).

In a similar vein, the various autobiographies and autobiographical essays of key activists of the period (Cleve Sellers, James Forman, Bobby Seale, Huey Newton, Amiri Baraka, Ron Karenga) as well as those accounts that can be considered objective (Harold Cruse, Stokely Carmichael, Manning Marable, Paula Giddings) reveal a process of development among activists that resembles the one in the fiction examined in this book. Many of the sources used for this study were written by individuals who were involved in creating the history dealt with here. Their autobiographical nature does not compromise their usefulness for understanding the sixties; rather, particularly in the cases of Karenga and Baraka, their involvement in the events about which they write helps in understanding their ability to deal with the opportunities and problems created by the activism of the sixties. Coupled with the journalistic and sociological references, these sources help to provide a full picture of that era.

Conflict resolution and the ability to move on after certain goals either have not been obtained or have been radically altered depends on the level of literacy achieved by the individual in question. Freedom and literacy are necessary for a fictive character or an individual in the real world to actualize his or her potential. The quest for freedom and literacy as a basis to analyze Afro-American life and literature is derived from a philosophical position that assumes the existence of a cultural memory intertwined with the activities of Afro-Americans. In this study, the actions of fictional characters and Afro-Americans in the real world are best understood as attempts to make sense of black involvement in Vietnam, the civil rights movement, and the black power movement. The actions of fictional characters and real-world individuals who are influenced by these three historical events can be classified as attempts to gain historical understanding (freedom) and the ability to use that understanding in ways consistent with the individual's personality (literacy).

From the foregoing, it should be clear that my critical method is a continuation and a refinement of the black aesthetic criticism of the sixties. It is a continuation in two ways and a refinement in one critical way. As a continuation, my method, like the black aesthetic mode of criticism, seeks to identify fundamental or paradigmatic aspects of Afro-American life that originate in the folk culture. Larry Neal, for example, an important theorist of black art, argued that it derived its form and meaning from black music and from the oral nature of Afro-American culture. Others, including Addison Gayle, Hoyt Fuller, and Carolyn Fowler, made similar arguments, generally noting that folk culture was the basis for determining the terms and modes of criticism of Afro-American literature. I believe that the quest for freedom and literacy is a useful concept to describe the interactions of Afro-Americans with the world, for it goes to the core of the motivational factors in the lives of most Afro-Americans. Artistic as well as other activities of Afro-Americans are best understood as attempts to advance the quest for freedom and literacy.

The second connection my method has to black aesthetic criticism is its assumption that all art has a political function intended in some way to clarify and advance the aesthetic or spiritual concerns of its culture's members. This advancement is not esoteric in the sense that it encourages withdrawal or singular contemplations of beauty by the supremely educated individual. Rather, the clarification and advancement of aesthetic/spiritual concerns is intended to influence the way members of a culture see the world. It is tantamount to the advancement of the quest for freedom and literacy. The political dimension of black aesthetic criticism is derived from the assumption that the way a culture conceptualizes the world determines choices it makes in dealing with the world's opportunities and pitfalls.

The refinement I offer to black aesthetic criticism involves accepting the philosophical assumptions of that criticism and offering operational definitions that minimize the chances of reductive criticism. Black aestheticians were criticized for being too proscriptive, often ignoring the formal aspects of the text in an effort to make political assessments about its relative "blackness." Indicating and defining paradigmatic motivational aspects of Afro-American life— freedom and literacy—maximizes the chances that the resulting criticism will be political; that is, that it will stipulate relationships between the development of a piece of creative literature and that of various aspects of Afro-American life. Here the area of confluence is the sixties, more specifically, black involvement in the Vietnam War and the civil rights and black power movements.

The attempt to do criticism from the perspective outlined above without reducing literature to a formula is accomplished by dealing with the formal aspects of literature. Plot, characterization, setting, theme, and so on are all useful markers for focusing attention on how the quest for freedom and literacy is or is not advanced. My focus here is on determining the extent to which plot and characterization in the novels I examine advance or fail to advance the quest for freedom and literacy.

My method is in contrast to the various current expressions of formalism, and that contrast is primarily a philosophical one. For me Afro-American literature is a political as opposed to a linguistic product. Therefore, criticism that ignores or discounts the political dimension of literature in preference for that literature's linguistic dimensions is not useful for connecting the life and literature of a people involved in the process of self-definition.

This book is divided into two sections, one concerned with black involvement in the Vietnam War and the other with the civil rights and black power movements. Each section is introduced by sociological, journalistic, and historical accounts of the problem, and this commentary is woven into the discussion of the novels when necessary to illuminate the social history they present. In discussing each novel I examine the way point of view and structure work to shape the development of characters in light of their involvement either in Vietnam, the civil rights movement, or the black power movement.

The central point I wish to illustrate through analyzing the impact of the activism of the sixties on Afro-American fictional characters and Afro-Americans in the real world is that the process involved in achieving freedom and literacy increases the chances that individuals will be able to resolve conflict. For it is an anchoring process, without which Afro-Americans, be they fictional or real, are adrift in a sea without markers.

Notes

1. For an excellent bibliography of this era see Carolyn Fowler, *Black Art and Black Aesthetics* (Atlanta: First World Publication, 1981).

2. In *From Behind the Veil*, Robert Stepto discusses W.E.B. DuBois's *Souls of Black Folk* as "a narrative of a cultural archetype . . . in that it identifies existing cultural expressions and postures far more than it imitates them . . . it is the first true expression of the Afro-American cultural immersion ritual" (66). My usage of the term *immersed* is similar to Stepto's in that I am also referring to archetypal patterns in the culture that, in a sense, precede linear conceptions of time. More specifically, immersion can be understood here to correspond to my definition of *freedom*, that is, knowledge of the racial memory.

3. Ron Karenga's "Overturning Ourselves: From Mystification to Meaningful Struggle," *Black Scholar*, October 1972, pp. 6–14, is an excellent analysis of ahistorical romanticism, particularly in its discussion of the consequences of the identification of that tendency in the organization Karenga headed (US) and of the consequences of that romanticism among activists.

References

Baker, Houston. *Blues, Ideology and Afro-American Literature: A Vernacular Theory*. Chicago: University of Chicago Press, 1984.

Baraka, Amiri. *The Autobiography of Leroi Jones*. New York: Freundlich Books, 1984.

Blassingame, John. *The Slave Community: Plantation Life in the Antebellum South*. New York: Oxford University Press, 1972.

Brown, Wesley. *Tragic Magic*. New York: Random House, 1978.

Carmichael, Stokely, and Charles V. Hamilton. *Black Power*. New York: Vintage Books, 1967.

Davis, George, and Glegg Wilson. *Black Life in Corporate America: Swimming in the Mainstream*. Garden City, N.Y.: Doubleday Anchor Books, 1985.

DuBois, W.E.B. *The Souls of Black Folk*. 1903. Reprint. New York: New American Library, 1969.

Forman, James. *The Making of a Black Revolutionary*. New York: Macmillan, 1971.

Frye, Northrop. *The Critical Path*. Bloomington: Indiana University Press, 1973.

Gates, Henry Louis, Jr., ed. *Black Literature and Literary Theory*, New York: Methuen, 1984.

Giddings, Paula. *When and Where I Enter: The Impact of Black Women on Race and Sex in America*. New York: Morrow, 1984.

Gwaltney, John Langston, comp. *Drylongso: A Self-Portrait of Black America*. New York: Random House, 1980.

Henderson, Stephen. *Understanding the New Black Poetry*. New York: Morrow, 1973.

Herskovits, Melville. *The Myth of the Negro Past*. Boston: Beacon Press, 1958.

Hurston, Zora Neale. *Mules and Men*. Philadelphia: Lippincott, 1935.

Killens, John. *The Cotillion, or One Good Bull Is Half the Herd*. New York: Trident Press, 1971.

Levine, Laurence. *Black Culture and Black Consciousness: Afro-American Folk Thought from Slavery to Freedom*. New York: Oxford University Press, 1977.

McCluskey, John. *Look What They Done to My Song*. New York: Random House, 1974.

Marable, Manning. *From the Grassroots: Social and Political Essays towards Afro-American Liberation*. Boston: South End Press, 1980.

Newton, Huey. *To Die for the People*. New York: Random House, 1972.

Reed, Ishmael. *The Last Days of Louisiana Red*. New York: Random House, 1974.

Seale, Bobby. *Seize the Time*. New York: Random House, 1970.

Sellers, Cleve. *River of No Return*. New York: Morrow, 1973.

Smitherman, Geneva. *Talkin and Testifyin*. New York: Houghton Mifflin, 1977.

Stepto, Robert. *From Behind the Veil: A Study of Afro-American Narrative*. Urbana: University of Illinois Press, 1979.

Toldson, Ivory, and Alfred D. Pasteur. *Roots of Soul*. Garden City, N.Y.: Doubleday Anchor Books, 1982.

Walker, Alice. *Meridian*. New York: Harcourt Brace Jovanovitch, 1976.

Williams, John A. *Captain Blackman*. Garden City, N.Y.: Doubleday, 1972.

PART I

Novels of the Vietnam War

1

Black Perspectives on Vietnam:
An Overview

What did Vietnam mean to Afro-American soldiers and civilians? When viewed through the fictive paradigm of three novels, *Captain Blackman* (John A. Williams), *Coming Home* (George Davis), and *Tragic Magic* (Wesley Brown), the effects of the war can be seen as occurring in three stages: (1) the soldiers are thrilled at the opportunity to prove their fighting skill; (2) they become disillusioned by the discriminatory practices of white peers and commanding officers; (3) finally, they commence a cultural-historical search for precedents that can help them make sense of their involvement.

Most of the soldiers portrayed in this fiction pass quickly through the first stage in this process. But many remain trapped between the first and second stages, aware that their actions will never earn them the respect of whites yet unable to break free of the need for a valuation that will never occur. Because soldiers in this category cannot generalize their predicament, they suffer from a self-alienation that prevents them from advancing the quest for freedom and literacy.

One of the most striking aspects of those characters caught between the first two stages of meaning is their tendency to adopt and apply the prejudices whites have toward blacks against Asians. Several of the black characters in *Captain Blackman* adopt racist stereotypes that see Vietnamese as "gooks" and make killing them a casual and commonplace occurrence. For example, Childress, a black pilot and associate of Ben, the protagonist in *Coming Home*, assumes that the medals he wins for killing "gooks" will serve as admission tickets to white America. These badges of courage will say, "I have arrived." Otis, Ellington's friend in *Tragic Magic*, loses a hand in Vietnam, but he can never reconcile his experience with the scenes of various John Wayne movies. Intellectually he knows the war is not like the celluloid projections of Hollywood, but emotionally he remains committed to fantasy. He never closes the gap between what he has been socialized to believe and what his experience has shown him. Because these characters are unable to discover precedents in Afro-American history that would help them understand their stay in Vietnam, they do not advance the quest for freedom and literacy.

For characters who commence a cultural-historical search—the third stage of meaning—the war experience is transformed into an opportunity to advance that quest. Blackman (*Captain Blackman*) achieves the transformation through historical study. For Ben (*Coming Home*), it becomes possible through reflection, and for Ellington (*Tragic Magic*), it is a metaphorical transformation, for he finds in jazz a cultural referent that can contain apparent contradictions.

Based on precedents in the rich history of blacks in the military Blackman decides to end the cycle of black exploitation by whites during times of war. Ben's decision is less dramatic, but still his desertion is cast in the framework of Afro-American history: the uncertainties of an audacious move—be it an attempt to escape from slavery or a move from the rural South to the urban North—are preferable to the certainties of a debilitating present. Ellington locates the center of himself through jazz, and for the first time in his life he is able to hear beneath discordant sounds ("sounds" is a metaphor for people's actions) and to reveal deeper harmonies. When he sees that antagonisms in either his personal or political life are complementary aspects of an ongoing dialectic in the black community he can move forward.

When characters achieve the third stage, the war is for them no longer an alienating experience. In the company of ancestors and others who are dealing with a similar set of problems, they become more than lonely individuals hanging from a curious and contradictory precipice. Tension is gone, and although its absence does not guarantee overt political activity, that absence is necessary for change to occur.

The fictional characters who discover themselves in aspects of Afro-American history that complement rather than distort their personalities achieve various degrees of freedom and literacy. Their knowledge of history provides a perspective that allows them to move beyond their present involvements and thereby gain a certain freedom. Additionally, when the history is personalized, made to serve their particular talents and idiosyncrasies, they achieve a degree of literacy.

Those characters caught between the first and second stages of meaning are unable to reflect on the meanings of their actions and those of the people around them because their conceptions of what is possible are limited by the degree of their socialization. Nor are they literate, for they cannot control their feelings and actions long enough to know what they like and dislike about themselves. Locating oneself in history requires a level of reflection that these characters lack.

The fictional characters who do not fight in Vietnam but are affected by the war experience a similar three-part process. This group, however, is similar to the second group discussed above, which fails to advance the quest for freedom and literacy. Those affected by the war but not fighting in it tend to slide into an existing niche of Americana, waiting for clarity to descend from the sky.

The three-part process that occurs in the fiction closely parallels events in the real world. To be sure, the black response to the war did not follow a straight path from optimism to disillusionment to search, but black involvement in the war as portrayed by mass-circulation newsmagazines and by some black leaders did follow a path similar to the one plotted above (Foner, 204–7). Although there was always strong and organized resistance to black involvement in the war, that opposition was not initially widely representative of the black community (Foner, 204; Mullen, 64).

During the early stages of the war, from 1963 until approximately 1967, the news media as well as many black leaders sought to characterize black involvement in the war as an indication of racial progress. Headlines in magazines announced the optimism felt by many Afro-Americans: "How Negro Americans Perform in Vietnam" (1966), "Guardians of the Vietnam Coastline" (1966), "Birdmen with Black Rifles; Screaming Eagle Paratroopers" (1966), "The Great Society in Uniform" (1966), and "Democracy in the Foxhole" (1967).

U.S. News and World Reports noted: "The combat performance of individual Negro troops in this war is equal to that of whites, as far as any reporter can tell. There are many examples of individual heroism by Negro infantrymen, and no broad indictments of Negro troops such as were heard in previous wars under a policy of segregated units" ("How Negro Americans Perform in Vietnam," 60). This quote is revealing in that it assumes the advantages of an integrated fighting force and for its view of black military history. Integration placed the black soldier on the same level as his white peers. This clearly improved situation made it unnecessary for black soldiers to deal with the contradictions they faced as a function of their identity as members of an oppressed race fighting for their oppressors. They were considered fortunate to be in a position to prove themselves. The quote also suggests that black military history, with all units segregated, was marked by incompetence and cowardice. The literature on this subject is replete with examples of black soldiers serving honorably in all of America's wars (Foner, Mullen). The contrary interpretation, in which propaganda supersedes truth, is an attempt to portray black involvement in Vietnam as a break from a cowardly tradition.

The propaganda of integration is continuous with the idea of progress in America, and progress as defined by those in power in this country is based on a linear interpretation that often results in historical amnesia. The news stories depicted the black soldiers in Vietnam as the first black soldiers in American military history to rise to the occasion. Many Afro-Americans accepted this propaganda and made bizarre statements that reflected their acceptance. George Shaffer, an Afro-American lieutenant colonel during the Vietnam War, said in reference to the high casualty rate among black soldiers: "I feel good about it. Not that I like bloodshed, but the performance of the Negro in Vietnam tends to offset the fact that the Negro wasn't considered worthy of being a first line soldier" (Foner, 205). The disproportionately high sacrifice of black bodies is a strange dowry to pay a country that has routinely disrespected black life, but Shaffer's view was not unique among black officers. Major Beauregard Brown said, "The notion has been disproved on the Vietnam battlefield . . . that Negroes can't produce the same as white soldiers. Given the same training and support, the Negro has shown that he can do the job just as good as anyone else" (Terry, 201). Gerald Snead discusses his experience with one black officer who had internalized the American Dream. Snead was given the choice of going back to federal prison or going to Vietnam. Here he describes the black man who gave him that choice:

> My eyes lifted from the floor to gaze at this man in black skin as he smiled painfully at the flag on his desk. i flashed on an old sister i remember seeing in church as a kid. She was on her knees looking up at a blue-eyed figure on a cross and asking for forgiveness. i wanted to cry for the captain as much as i wanted to destroy him. Here was a brother who had lied about his age to join the service twenty years ago, probably because he never had any thing anyway and, by becoming a soldier, he would earn respect that was denied him and his people since the beginning of slavery. He would show the world that he could kill as good as any white man, whoever the "enemy" was, whether gook, kraut, or nigger. (Snead, 234)

Snead's account is instructive in showing the extent to which some black officers had bought into the system. As the war progressed, however, it became easy to find black officers who were quite eloquent in their condemnation of the war and of the use to which black soldiers were put.

General William Westmoreland, the commander of U.S. troops in Vietnam, praised Afro-American soldiers as "courageous on the battlefield, proficient and possessor[s] of technical skills" (Foner, 205). Westmoreland felt no need to connect these traits to the Afro-American military tradition. The *New York Times* showed more perspective on the issue when it reported that "Vietnam gives lie to the official policy of prejudice by the military establishment in two wars" (Foner, 205). This affirmation of equality, though more continuous with black military history than the comments of Shaffer, Brown, and Westmoreland, said nothing of the contradiction the black soldier faced.

During the early stages of the war, black enlisted men thought fighting in Vietnam was the American thing to do. One such soldier said, "Negroes should be used in this war because the United States consists of Negroes and whites." Another soldier similarly stated, "I don't think King and Carmichael are right [a reference to their protest against the war]. They live in a free country and somebody has to pay for it" (Terry, 203). For these soldiers, their blackness was mere happenstance. Historical amnesia, the clear result of socialization, was in place and functioning.

Another aspect of historical amnesia is illustrated in the racist stereotypes of blacks depicted in popular magazines. These stereotypes, based on a limited perspective of Afro-American history, were trotted out either to demonstrate that the war could work to destroy the shackles they imposed or to justify the disproportionate number of blacks killed in the war. A 1967 *Time* magazine article, for example, took the "black matriarch" stereotype derived from Patrick Moynihan's work as accepted fact: "He [the black soldier] may fight to prove his manhood—perhaps as a corrective to the matriarchial dominance of the Negro—to shatter stereotypes of racial inferiority, to win the judgements of noncoms and officers of whatever color" ("Democracy in the Foxhole," 15). The opportunity to expand beyond the false boundaries of stereotypes resulting from white racism demonstrates how black military history was made to yield to the demands of propaganda.

Ebony, a mass-circulation black publication, also slipped into the use of stereotypes on occasion. The magazine explained the disproportionate number of blacks in the paratroopers: "Because of the Negro's ready adaptability to jungle warfare, they essentially are the backbone of the military thrust in Viet Nam" ("Birdmen with Black Rifles," 37). That *Ebony* could slip so easily into racist assessments of black capabilities (their ready adaptability to jungle warfare is a specific application of an Archie Bunkerish "jungle bunny" mentality) illustrates a certain area of black thinking concerning black involvement in Vietnam. A black publication, normally current on symbolic blackness, blandly cheered the progress and opportunity the war offered the black soldier.

Racial harmony and the various blessings of integration also saturated reports about black involvement in the war. A 1967 *New York Times* article reports: "The American ground forces are almost free of racial tension, and most soldiers—Negro and white—appear proud of this" (Foner, 203). The media were unanimous on this issue: "Reporters for newspapers, magazines, and television alike sent back glowing accounts on the harmonious race relations that existed in the integrated fighting forces. Close living and the common sharing of dangers, they claimed, had cemented friendships and mutual respect between whites and blacks" (Foner, 203). Although much of this propaganda ignored indicators of emerging problems—"The fact that once off the battlefield, blacks and whites continued to congregate in separate groups was attributed to personal choice rather than imposed segregation" (Foner, 203)—there were also many signs that blacks found the military a good opportunity.

The level at which Afro-Americans reenlisted and the rate at which they volunteered for hazardous duty suggested that they saw the war as a chance to improve their lives. Black reenlistment rates were at least twice as high as those for whites in the air force, navy, and marines and about three times as high in the army (Foner, 204). Although for many of them, these decisions were based on economics—the soldiers received bonuses for reenlisting and incentive pay for hazardous duty—there was also a pride that accompanied serving in elite units.

As noted earlier, however, a strain of discontent ran parallel with and ultimately replaced the early optimism concerning black involvement in Vietnam: "The first organized protest took the form of a leaflet circulated in McComb, Mississippi, and printed in the Mississippi Freedom Democratic Party Newsletter of McComb on July 28, 1965. The statement said, in part: 'It is very easy to understand why Negro citizens of McComb, themselves the victims of bombings, Klan inspired terrorism, and harassment, arrest, should resent the death of a citizen of McComb while fighting in Vietnam for "freedom" not enjoyed by the Negro community in McComb' " (Mullen, 68). By 1966 the Student Non-Violent Coordinating Committee (SNCC) and the Southern Christian Leadership Conference (SCLC) had come out against the war (Mullen, 69; Foner, 206). At the time, however, they were in the minority within the black community. According to a 1966 *Newsweek* poll, only 35 percent of Afro-Americans opposed the war. By late 1968 and into 1969, the black community's position had shifted. *Newsweek* conducted another poll in 1968, and it revealed that 56 percent of the Afro-American community opposed the war (Mullen, 64).

Titles of articles in newsmagazines signaled the shift in the nation's attitude regarding black involvement in the war: "Paradox of the Black Soldier" (1968), "Black Power in Vietnam" (1969), "The Military Meets the Afro" (1970), and " 'Pound,' A New Unity Sign; Ritual Greeting of Black Soldiers in Vietnam" (1971) are representative.

By 1970–71, the reality of black involvement in the war as reflected by the disproportionate number of black soldiers assigned to hazardous duty and killed made it impossible for blacks to support the war. On this issue Robert Mullen writes: "While blacks were generally no more than 11% of the total enlisted personnel in Vietnam they comprised 15% of all army units, and in army combat units the proportion was higher. In terms of casualties, blacks suffered nearly 17% of all deaths in Vietnam between 1961 and 1967 although the percentage of black troops in Southeast Asia was around 12%. In 1970, while they were 11% of the troops in Vietnam, blacks took 22% of the casualties" (Mullen, 77). In 1971 the Black Congressional Caucus investigated racism in the military and found, among other things, that black soldiers failed to win key command posts, often received indifferent medical treatment, and received a disproportionately low number of honorable discharges. One of the more interesting findings by the caucus in illustrating the consequences of black soldiers viewing themselves in the context of Afro-American history was that they suffered harassment and intimidation and were given the most dangerous combat assignments when they wore Afro hairstyles or used black power symbols or showed signs of militancy (*Time*, 29 November 1971). As these soldiers moved toward the third aspect of the three-part movement—a cultural-historical search to locate historical precedents—they achieved various degrees of freedom and literacy.

Black soldiers who achieved a degree of freedom and literacy were forthright in their comments concerning their place in America's war: " 'When you come back to the states and the Man's going to say, "Sorry, Son, but, I'm going to give you these rights, but you ain't ready for the rest of them yet," after I put my life on the line. Uh-Uh. . . . The man who says that, I'm going to try to kill him. If I can't kill him, he's going to wish he were dead' " (Terry, 206). Echoing a similar sentiment, another soldier said, " 'My ancestors said please. Yea, they said please. Did they get any mercy? Why should we turn around and say please, may I have this. Hell no. I say start the armed revolution' " (Terry, 207). These men are representative of the no longer alienated black soldier who sees himself functioning in a historical arena over which he exercises some control.

Another measure of change is reflected in the way some black officers who had made the military a career saw black involvement: " 'When I came into the Army in 1956, everything was quiet. . . . No one was raising hell about the prejudice and discrimination that was going on. The Negro soldier didn't know which way to go as far as speaking out against it. Now they can speak and somebody will listen. And some feel that since they are going to face death, it doesn't matter what he says' " (Terry, 210–11). This black officer's view does not reflect the historical amnesia and optimism demonstrated in the quotes from officers who spoke during the initial phase of black involvement.

Soldiers such as the ones quoted above were drafted after 1967 and had participated in urban rebellions; some had been members of the Black Panther party or US (Terry, 212–13). Consequently, they never saw the military as an opportunity to prove themselves worthy Americans. Nevertheless, they were forced to discover ways of relieving the psychological tension their presence in Vietnam created. The demands of these soldiers for magazines and books depicting black life indicates their desire to discover precedents that would allow self-comprehension.

The military responded predictably to the demands of these soldiers. The first response was to deny them, correctly reasoning that a historically conscious Afro-American soldier could not be depended on to do this country's fighting. But as national and international resistance to the war grew, the military acquiesced. Natural hairstyles were allowed, and as a measure of progress, military barbers were taught the intricacies of its care. In military mess halls, soul food was on the menu and a series of commercials appeared, letting blacks know that, among other things, they could be "black and navy too." All of these accommodations were gasps from a failing war machine riddled with morale problems and almost universal criticism for its conduct in Vietnam.

The movement of fictive and real-life characters through the three stages—the desire to prove fighting skill so as to be thought American, the subsequent disillusionment occasioned by the experience of racism, and the cultural-historical search for clarifying precedents—shows interactions among worlds useful in determining how Afro-Americans in the world dealt with the contradictions of the war. The novels analyzed in this first part of the book will show how Afro-Americans affected by Vietnam advanced or failed to advance the quest for freedom and literacy.

References

Anthony, F.C. " 'Pound,' A New Unity Sign; Ritual Greeting of Black Soldiers in Vietnam." *America* 124 (13 February 1971): 1478.

"Armed Forces: Black Powerlessness." *Time*, 29 November 1971, pp. 24–26.

"Birdmen with Black Rifles; Screaming Eagle Paratroopers." *Ebony*, October 1966, pp. 37–42.

"Black Power in Vietnam." *Time*, 19 September 1969, pp. 22–23.

Brown, Wesley. *Tragic Magic*. New York: Random House, 1978.

Davis, George. *Coming Home*. New York: Random House, 1971.

"Democracy in the Foxhole." *Time*, 26 May 1967, pp. 15–19.

Foner, Jack D. *Blacks and the Military in American History*. New York: Praeger, 1974.

"Great Society in Uniform." *Newsweek*, 22 August 1966, pp. 45–57.

"Guardians of the Vietnam Coastline." *Ebony*, December 1966, pp. 129–30.

"How Negro Americans Perform in Vietnam: With Chart." *U.S. News and World Report*, 15 August 1966, pp. 60–63.

Johnson, Thomas H. "Negroes in the Nam." *Ebony*, August 1968, pp. 32–36.

"The Military Meets the Afro." *Ebony*, September 1970, pp. 86–92.

Morris, Steve. "How Blacks Upset the Marine Corps." *Ebony*, December 1969, pp. 86–92.

Mullen, Robert W. *Blacks in American Wars*. New York: Monad Press, 1973.

"One War: Negro Disillusionment with Vietnam." *Nation*, 14 October 1967, p. 357.

"Paradox of the Black Soldier." *Ebony*, August 1968, p. 142.

"Report from Black America—A *Newsweek* Poll." *Newsweek*, 30 June 1969, pp. 16–35.

"Soul Alley, Home for Black AWOLS and Deserters." *Time*, 14 December 1970, pp. 39–40.

Snead, Gerald. "Vietnam: A Brother's Account." In *Vietnam and Black America*, edited by Clyde Taylor. Garden City, N.Y.: Doubleday Anchor Books, 1973. Pp. 233–42.

Terry, Wallace II. "Bringing the War Home." In *Vietnam and Black America*, edited by Clyde Taylor. Garden City, N.Y.: Doubleday Anchor Books, 1973. Pp. 200–219.

Williams, John A. *Captain Blackman*. Garden City, N.Y.: Doubleday, 1972.

2

Captain Blackman
and Cultural Literacy

The tradition that John A. Williams develops in *Captain Blackman* provides insight into two important aspects of black involvement in Vietnam: he illustrates the social and psychological factors necessary to understanding why black soldiers join the military in the first place; and he presents the relationship between historical understanding and the characters' perception of their involvement in Vietnam. The first insight highlights the contradictory nature of black involvement in all American wars. The exploration of this contradiction gives us some understanding as to why Afro-Americans were initially thrilled at the opportunity to prove themselves in Vietnam. Their titillation can be understood as a form of double-consciousness, that sense of simultaneously belonging and not belonging to American society (DuBois). The soldiers felt their service in the military could act as a bridge, however ephemeral, to connect the American and African halves of themselves and assure acceptance by white America.

There is a long tradition of optimism of this nature, usually labeled "acculturation or accommodation" (Meier, 69–82), and it was certainly operative during the Vietnam War era. In a 1967 article, Morris Jonowitz, a sociologist from the University of Chicago, asserts in an interview that "the experience of the military will integrate them [black veterans] into the larger society. They will be more likely to enter the mainstream of political American life" ("Democracy in the Foxhole," 19). During the early phases of the war, many black soldiers echoed similar sentiments: "I want to emphasize that race is simply not germane here"; "We're all treated equal in the corps—white, black, German or Jewish"; "Over here its different. A war's on. There's no room for prejudice" ("How Negroes Perform in Vietnam," 62–63). These soldiers' feelings imply that the military is a model from which the overall society might learn. Jack Foner notes that "during the mid-1960s most black military personnel and civilians had a decidedly favorable opinion of the armed forces. They considered the military establishment the most completely integrated segment of American society and the one that provided the best career opportunity for black men" (Foner, 204). An Afro-American observer makes a similar point: "The military establishment is hailed as being one of the most democratic institutions in America" (Terry, 210). This person ultimately asserts that the military establishment is not democratic, although he admits that many blacks perceived it as a democratic institution. Certainly the young Blackman did not give racism in the military a thought; for him an army career seemed an excellent opportunity.

The comments by Jonowitz and by black soldiers and Foner indicate a historical amnesia about the contradictory nature of Afro-American existence, which is best understood as an expression of double-consciousness. Jonowitz ignores the efforts of black men and women to "enter the mainstream of political American life." They are not held back from making such moves by reticence or reluctance but by the ingenious forms of white racism. Instead of looking at the entire history on the subject, Jonowitz focuses on the victim of racism—the black man—and implies that the victim is responsible for not being part of the mainstream. Those ebullient black soldiers quoted were either affected by historical amnesia or so anxious to belong in the mainstream that they were unable to generalize the black experience in Vietnam. From my perspective the Foner quote illustrates a similar phenomenon: the characterization of the military as a democratic institution is derived from the American half of double-consciousness. For it is that half which places a high priority on belonging; as various segments of the Afro-American community were to learn and still continue to learn, however, any resolution of the dilemma of double-consciousness is not static or event-oriented.

A black woman or man can never accumulate enough accomplishments to assure white America's acceptance; thus any solution to the dilemma resides in acknowledging it as a dynamic process, the rules of which are always open to change. A successful negotiating of trips around the poles of double-consciousness has to be charted as an attempt to achieve freedom and literacy. Specifically, knowledge of the racial memory and its individualized application is at the center of successfully dealing with the contradiction of double-consciousness. Those characters who do not realize this fail to advance the quest for freedom and literacy and therefore live bitter and confused lives.

The second insight is the relationship between historical understanding and the way characters perceive their involvement in Vietnam. Abraham Blackman demonstrates that characters who see themselves as functioning within a historical tradition are critical of the war. Generally, the more historical understanding a given character has, the more critical he is of the war. Because the novel is an allegory, Blackman's understanding leads to an ultimate solution that is intended to end the contradictory nature of black military involvement in American wars and in effect destroy the basis for this specific manifestation of double-consciousness. If there is no "white" military, blacks will not need or want to prove themselves within that structure. Blackman devises a method to render inoperative America's defense system of enemy missile detection, and he prepares to launch a military attack from a West African nation.

The audacity of this plan, especially in light of its actual or even textual credibility, is a direct result of the historical literacy Blackman achieves. This novel, more than the others treated here, demonstrates the consequences of historical understanding to the way Afro-Americans perceived their Vietnam involvement. In this sense, the novel provides an enlightening way of viewing the various cultural demands that black soldiers made during the Vietnam War, for these demands were attempts on the part of the soldiers to discover themselves in the context of Afro-American history.

The novel's narrative structure reflects Williams's desire to correct the record of black military history. Accordingly, he uses historical documents, and he provides conversations between fictional characters and historical personalities such as Andrew Jackson and Dwight Eisenhower. Together, these two techniques have the effect of undercutting accepted interpretations of historical events and forcing the reader to consider the validity of the interpretations that can be deduced from the novel's narrative.

The sections that use historical documents are labeled "Drumtaps," and they both underscore the heroism of the black soldier and illustrate the unjust treatment to which he is subjected. The sections that relate motives of white characters are labeled "Cadences" and usually occur near the beginning of a chapter. This structural placement of the "Cadences" also works to foreshadow action.

Whites' motives for starting wars are portrayed as an interaction between racism and greed. For example, a group of industrialists and soldiers discusses the need to expand the railroad from east to west. The Indians stand in the way of this project, but the solution is simple: " 'Gentlemen, taking the lesson from our British cousins, we're merely employing one group of natives, the niggers, to fight another group of natives, the Indians. The strategy has met with marked success in British dominance' " (Williams, 96).

As the novel progresses, America's racism and imperialism harden to preclude an accurate perception of Afro-American capabilities. Once he leaves the service Blackman trains blacks in Sub-Saharan Africa to destroy America's defense systems. The novel ends with that goal accomplished and General Ishmael Whitman, the principal white protagonist, remarking bemusedly that the "niggers have finally won." The fantastic method of obtaining retribution is equal to the historical exclusion of black military achievement from the public record. Indeed, given Williams's concerns, that absence, to be balanced, must be countered by a final solution. The allegory requires that freedom and literacy be expressed in a concrete form that will end the contradiction of double-consciousness.

Given the American military tradition, which is characterized by outright exploitation on the part of white commanders and white peers, why did black soldiers join the military to fight in Vietnam? In Blackman's case—and surely Williams intends us to understand this character as every "Black Man"—there are two interrelated reasons: an absence of life choices usually resulting from economic constraints and a pervasive socialization process that suggests to young black men that the military is a democratic institution in which advancements result from merit and not race.

Blackman's parents are not wealthy, and they are divorced.

Though we know relatively little about them, it is clear that they are too trapped within their own insecurities to play an instructive role in their son's development. His mother is a "frightened woman who lets the world cope with her because she was unable to cope with it." His father moves with similar detachment, occasionally mumbling to his son about ways of coping with life's changes. Phrases like Do the right thing or Do what makes you happy swirl throughout Blackman's confusing adolescence. Neither parent comments when he quits high school football and track—activities that could have earned him an athletic scholarship to a university—to become a boxer; nor do they say anything when their son's boxing career is cut short by a powerful "haymaker." Though the book is an allegory, Blackman's parents are very much in the tradition of the realist character in Afro-American literature. They do not reflect on the meanings of events that have shaped their lives, so life for them is one-dimensional, a series of stimuli to which they mechanically respond. Lacking the ability to reflect, they experience everything as if for the first time. Encased in their own narrow notions of what is possible, they cannot help their son.

After high school the young Blackman leaves Binghamton, New York, his hometown, for New York City, hoping to acquire direction for his life. Once in New York he works at various jobs, thinks of going to college eventually; and fights frequent battles with restlessness and a "distressing ennui." Thus at eighteen, without parental guidance or an ability to pull any useful precedent from Afro-American history, Blackman makes a convenient decision. He joins the army: "Three squares, a profession and travel and rapid promotion. He left New York without looking back" (Williams, 297).

Although this part of the novel is set in the fifties, the social landscape that makes the military an option for Blackman is similar to that which attracted black men eligible for the draft during the Vietnam era. In Wallace Terry's *Bloods*, numerous black veterans discuss their rationale for joining the military. Reginald "Malik" Edwards's explanation is representative: "I was the first person in my family to finish high school. This was 1963. I knew I couldn't go to college because my folks couldn't afford it. I only weighed 117 pounds, and nobody's gonna hire me to work for them. So the only thing left to do was go into the service" (Terry, *Bloods*, 6). Nowhere in

Edwards's recollections is there an indication that he truly believed the military would treat him fairly. But he had no other alternative, and the military seemed to be his best hope. Edwards and others in his situation sometimes feel a need to justify the military choice beyond expediency, and when they do, they find that there are innumerable images in the culture which the military exploits. The most pervasive Euro-American archetype of the black man is a conglomeration of negative images: he is lazy, untrustworthy, cowardly, bestial, and irresponsible. These images are so deeply embedded in Euro-American culture that industrious, honest, heroic, loving, and responsible black men are considered anomalies. The military exploits the archetype to suggest that the armed forces offer black men a chance at last to join the ranks of men.

Corroborating this view, albeit from a different angle, Alvin Poussaint writes: " 'Because of the limited opportunities that a racist society offers a black man for achieving manhood, I think many young black men gravitate to the Army to prove they are men by risking their lives in combat. Superior power in combat is one of the oldest ways of achieving a sense of manhood. The black man in combat is ready to trade his life for psychological manhood, status and self-esteem' " (Llorens, 88). A news correspondent of the Vietnam War era writing in 1967 makes a similar point: " 'Prestige units, combat units enable the young Negro soldier to prove himself and in his mind to others he is a man among men' " (Foner, 204–5). In *Captain Blackman* and in many instances in the real world, young black men who join the military feeling that the experience will make them men or that it will allow them to prove themselves men are disappointed. A sense of manhood must be based on some understanding of one's history and culture. The military is not capable of providing this understanding except by default.

To function, the military must acknowledge only that history which is useful to its maintenance and, when at war, useful to winning. Generally, this is accomplished by stressing cultural artifacts that are assumed to be common to the experience of its constituents. "Indeed, many soldiers argue that too many commanders had no appreciation 'of the uniqueness' of different ethnic groups but felt that 'the only color of a serviceman' was that of his green uniform" (Foner, 215). The military's necessary historical reductivism means that there is little chance that it can provide the black man with a sense of manhood.

Although Blackman's decision to join the military illustrates an essentially negative aspect of what it means to be a black man during time of war, the way he ultimately uses his war experience provides insight into the way the war could advance the quest for freedom and literacy. Blackman's development is an example of what happens to a soldier when he is able to generalize his experience through historical or cultural study.

Blackman's process of development mirrors the process outlined in the introduction to this section: he is first thrilled at the prospect of being in the military; he is then disillusioned as a result of the racist treatment he receives; and finally he commences a cultural search in an effort to locate himself in Afro-American history and thereby make some sense of his war experience. It is this last phase that is of importance here. Blackman's search is twofold: first, he needs racial fraternization to create a sense of well-being and self-worth; and second, he begins to study, primarily by holding conversations with old black veterans. These two activities light the way to understanding the cultural demands of blacks who fought in Vietnam and thereby illustrate a relationship between historical understanding and the way individuals thought about their own Vietnam experience.

In Japan Blackman experiences racial fraternization for an extended period, for there he meets and interacts with his first group of historically conscious black men, who spend their spare time together in an attempt to create a community similar to the one they knew in the United States. On the weekends "groups of the brothers got together with their Japanese girls and got into records, home food or just partying." These apparently innocuous activities replicate their experiences at home and in that way provide the basis for politicization in the form of discussions that seek to place the individual's immediate situation into a historical context. Racial fraternization did not always lead to politicization, but it was certainly a prerequisite for it and created a basis for freedom and literacy.

Being with friends provides a peaceful psychological base from which Blackman views the sporadic fights between black and white soldiers. These fights remind him that although both groups are soldiers, members of the same armed forces, and American citizens, they are still separate. In itself, this is not problematic; his being in the army and in Japan lets Blackman know that he belongs to American culture. But the unequal treatment that the black soldier receives lets him know that he does not truly belong. This realization is later nurtured through historical study and reflection, which provide Blackman with a single and clear consciousness that does not vacillate between a desire to belong and a desire not to belong to America. Blackman's new consciousness demands that the cycle of black exploitation be ended by a definitive act, the destruction of America. It is significant that fraternization with other black soldiers stimulated the formation of Blackman's consciousness.

Fraternization among black soldiers was commented on in passing during the early stages of the war and was generally thought a curious anomaly not worthy of concern. A 1967 *Time* magazine article is typical:

> Many Negroes prefer to pull their passes in Saigon's self-segregated Soulville, a warren of bases and brothels along Khanh Hoi Street near the capital waterfront. In the honky tonks, they can dig the big beat of the Supremes singing "Come See About Me" or the kinky cool of Ahmed Jamal's "Heat Wave," bop about the bars in their slacks and talk trash. The girls of Soulville—dark skinned Cambodians or the daughters of French-Senegalese soldiers—are less costly and usually less comely than are their sisters in white-dominated TuDo Street nearby. ("Democracy in the Foxhole," 17)

The writer sees black soldiers' creation of their own community during off-duty hours merely as theater. And his casual racism concerning the color and relative "comeliness" of prostitutes is but another indication of the lack of significance given to fraternization among black soldiers. For the writer, reality is the performance of the soldier on the battlefield. It was not until the black political climate changed from joy at the possibility of proving oneself a man to a criticism born from historical study that the military became concerned about black soldiers fraternizing.

Blackman's political consciousness is born within the context of off-duty fraternization. Williams's decision to write an allegory relieves him of the necessity of making the motivations and actions of the characters credible as they would have to be in a realist novel. So Blackman's development at the point in the novel when he begins to be disillusioned is best understood as expressing Williams's desire to demonstrate the relationship between historical understanding and militancy. The new Blackman, though not fully developed, considers a friend's love of the army. The Korean War provides the occasion for his reflection: "Now it's pay off time. Send your ass across the Yalu to stop 700 million Chinese who don't give a shit about you any more than you give a shit about them, just to save the world from communism for some whitey son of a bitch who's afraid of it because maybe it'd give other people the same things he has." The New Blackman condemns what he perceives as American imperialism. But he still has to deal with his failure to discover the bedrock of himself: "Blackman decided if he got through, he was going into the reserves, try to hold on to his grade, go to college. There was so much shit going on, he thought, I had to make some effort to understand it" (Williams, 305). In the world he confronts after Korea blacks are becoming increasingly militant. He does not know where he fits. He joins the reserves and uses the military as a base from which to launch his forays into historical and self-understanding. His initial approach is to acquire the external trappings of bourgeois society. He returns to New York City and enrolls in City College but never finishes; he marries but quickly learns that his new bride is not right for him because she wants a traditional middle-class existence. He gets a job with a Negro insurance company which fizzles when he learns that dismissals are more common than promotions.

The questions and problems that made the military seem appealing to the eighteen-year-old Blackman remain to haunt the adult. He has succeeded only in wrapping himself in traditional bourgeois activities and then in unwrapping himself from them. The effect is dizzying, and he gravitates again to the military, an obvious anchor.

When Blackman returns to active duty, he is made second lieutenant, guaranteed travel, and promised a promotion. He periodically returns stateside and is shaken by what he sees: "Martin King kept marching. John F. Kennedy was murdered. Malcolm X was murdered. Things were happening back home and the young Brothers were coming into the Army bad, not grateful anymore; if they ever were; not taking shit anymore. America was a strange place when he returned, just before his first hitch in Nam and he was glad to be out of it" (Williams, 313). Blackman is being shaped by the political climate in America, and his desire to get back to the military, the one environment he feels he understands, is similar to the naiveté we saw in him as an eighteen-year-old. The trips to America do upset him, however, and make him wonder. The final transformation of Blackman comes as a result of his talks with black veterans: "During his travels he'd met old vets from World War I; that old guy with the 369th near New Rochelle. Jesus, the army must've been a bitch for a black then, he thought. And the guy living in Stockholm who'd fought in Spain. And in Genoa he heard of Tombolo" (Williams, 312). Williams uses flashbacks to dramatize black involvement in these various wars.

The average Afro-American soldier did not have the opportunity to travel and talk with black soldiers from other wars, but many did seek to establish a link with the past through reading material and music. In isolation, the black soldier's demands for black reading material, music, and food are not extraordinary; they seem a standard response of any soldier fighting away from home. Unlike most American soldiers, however, the Afro-American is more likely to find the rhythms of the military foreign to those he is used to. A functioning army tends to obscure cultural differences and nuances among its members in favor of an assumed reservoir of shared experiences. This effacing of uniqueness made the Afro-American experience appear insignificant or invisible. Hillbilly and rock music, for example, were much more available and accessible than soul music (Foner, 209). The demands of black soldiers for Afrocentric reading material, music, and other cultural artifacts represented an attempt to escape from the immediate reality of Vietnam and to link themselves with an African or Afro-American tradition.

For Blackman, the traditions of his culture emerge as he studies black military history. More specifically, once he studies and understands the cycle of betrayal that black soldiers have undergone, he is compelled to launch an Armageddon in an effort to break the cycle. It is doubtful that black soldiers in Vietnam considered any retribution as absolute as that theorized by the fictional Blackman, but an abundance of evidence indicates a relationship between cultural historical understanding and militancy. That is, those Afro-American soldiers who were most conscious of their culture and history were less likely to accept the discriminatory practices of white peers and commanders than were those who on an unarticulated level saw themselves only as Americans.

Clinched-fist salutes, Afro hairstyles, and specific socializing patterns were among the clearest symbolic expressions of Afro-American cultural-historical identity. The various symbolic gestures of brotherhood originated and were enriched within the warm confines of racial fraternization, and their power is clear from the angry response of white enlisted men and officers. Staff sergeant Bobby Edwards of Woodsboro, Texas, said in 1970 concerning the clinched-fist salute: " 'They shouldn't make that sign. That is a show of rebellion and strength.' " A black soldier recalled that in response to a clinched-fist salute made by a black soldier to a black officer, his white commanding officer yelled at the black soldier: " 'What's this clinched fist mean? That sergeant [the black officer] is a good man. You're just a black nigger' " (Terry, "Bringing the War Home," 212).

Military policy did not always restrict the symbolic shows of racial solidarity and brotherhood among black soldiers, but restrictive attitudes need not be part of stated policy to have the desired effect. One black officer remarked: " 'I had an Afro cut. But I went through hell wearing it. So I shaved my head bald' " (Terry, "Bringing the War Home," 213). In 1969 the military tolerated long-haired white soldiers, but blacks with long hair, or those whose appearance or actions illustrated their racial, historical, and cultural uniqueness, were treated as undesirables. The military understood that black soldiers who consciously operated within their own cultural framework would rapidly see the contradiction of their participation in the war and become less manageable. As the white officer quoted above stated about the black power salute, it was " 'a show of rebellion and strength.' " We cannot speculate about the white officer's understanding of the ramifications of his words, but it is clear that black soldiers who expressed their cultural framework through such symbols as clinched-fist salutes and one hundred ways of shaking hands ("Black Power in Vietnam") were more likely to redress the effects of discrimination than were those who did not function within such a framework.

Black soldiers who were sent to Vietnam in the late sixties and early seventies were unlike those who went to the war earlier. The fictional Blackman "watched them [the new black recruits] change the army; their language seeped through everything, officers copied their idiom, so they could communicate better" (Williams, 313). Reports by correspondents during the late sixties stressed the change in attitude among many black servicemen, at home and abroad: "These men are a new generation of black soldiers. Unlike the veterans of a year or two ago, they are immersed in black awareness and racial pride. Although the military ascribed this development to attitudes blacks brought with them into the service from civilian society, one observer insisted: 'Despite command pronouncements to the contrary most of the rise of black consciousness within the armed forces seems to have occurred after service entry rather than as a spillover from civilian values' " (Foner, 207). The new Afro-American soldier, be he made in America or Vietnam, clearly was more straightforward and therefore problematic than his predecessor. This new black soldier was not content to wait for justice when he felt his rights had been violated. The MauMaus and the JuJus are excellent examples. Both groups functioned as "black protectives . . . against white prejudice and intimidation." A JuJu member explained that " 'the white man won't mess over us if we stick together.' " A MauMau member asserted that " 'if you're not tight with the brothers in the 'Nam, you can't get over' " (Terry, "Bringing the War Home," 214).

Their naming of the "black protectives" after black African freedom fighters is indicative of the cultural and historical understanding these black soldiers had achieved. Like their African brothers, they were engaged in a battle for self-definition and, to the extent that their highly contradictory involvement in the war would allow, a battle for self-determination. Although the MauMaus and JuJus did not have the benefit of Blackman's travel experience, they did manage to leave the realm of individual experience and form historically conscious organizations that were intended to assist them in defining and controlling their lives.

By the time Blackman returns to Vietnam, the military no longer benignly accepts the fraternization among black soldiers or the ritual greetings and other cultural expressions. In 1967 *Time* could lamely discuss black soldiers listening to "the big beat of the Supremes singing 'Come See About Me,' " but in 1969 the magazine entitled an article "Black Power in Vietnam." Fraternization had become the basis for politicization.

Wallace Terry noted: "In rear areas black soldiers, attracted by common music, language or hate live when they can in all black hootches, like the 'Little Ghetto,' 'Hekalu' in Chu Lai, and 'Hootch 8' in Cam Ranh Bay. Ron Karenga's Swahili-speaking US movement for black culture, pride and self-defense has spread to at least four Marine and Army bases in I Corps. And in Bien Hoa and Cam Ranh Bay, the Black Panthers in army uniforms have circulated their party literature" (Terry, "Bringing the War Home," 213). The names the soldiers chose for their "hootches," particularly "Little Ghetto," indicate their lack of interest in fitting into the American military fabric. By extension, it is clear that these men were also not interested in proving themselves worthy of respect.

Terry also notes other instances of cultural-historical activity among black soldiers: "Heggs [a black soldier in Vietnam], on his own time and theirs, taught black history to black and white airmen, soldiers and sailors in the Danang area. At Tan My and Bien Hoa, black sailors and airmen meet regularly to plan black cultural events and discuss their mutual problems" (Terry, "Bringing the War Home," 216).

One of the most eloquent examples of the use of symbols by black soldiers in Vietnam to advance racial solidarity and thereby make the war experience less alienating and senseless is described as follows: "In Danang, black Marines have designed a flag for black soldiers in Vietnam. A red background symbolizes blood shed by blacks in the war and in race conflict in America. A black foreground represents the face of black culture. At the center are crossed spears and a shield, meaning 'violence if necessary,' surrounded by a wreath, symbolizing 'peace if possible.' The flag bears a legend in Swahili, meaning 'My fear is for you' " (Terry, "Bringing the War Home," 214). As was the case with the choice of African names for the self-protection organizations, the use of Swahili to assert brotherhood indicates historical and cultural consciousness. Cultural and historical knowledge first finds symbolic manifestation in names, gestures, and other actions and artifacts. In some instances, the symbols seem an end in themselves, a psychological salve necessary to provide peace of mind and self-esteem. But in other instances, particularly in the case of the MauMaus and the JuJus, these symbols are the basis for actions directed toward self-defense and a necessarily circumscribed quest for self-determination. The symbols and the actions they sometimes inspire spring from a fundamental desire to make sense of a contradictory situation and thus become more profound than mere protest.

The complaints of some soldiers about being in Vietnam were

most concerned with eliminating barriers to full equality. The perspective of this group dominated the early stages of the war and can best be understood as belonging to the integrationist school of thought. But those soldiers who sought through their symbols and actions to establish an Afro-American beachhead from which to understand their presence in Vietnam were not protesting for inclusion. They felt distaste for the war itself. Thus the turning to and embellishing of indigenous forms is best understood as a nationalist quest for meaning and definition.

Noting the change, Foner writes: "Traditionally blacks had demanded complete equality of treatment within the armed forces— a demand which had been equated with integration and the idea that blacks should be treated exactly the same as whites. Now, just as this demand seemed close to fulfillment, black service men were demanding an official recognition of their distinctive life-style and culture" (Foner, 207). Foner's observations trace the development of the black soldier from optimism to pessimism to reflection or action, the three stages that describe the Afro-American reaction to service in Vietnam. By the time the soldiers reached the final stage of development, they could no longer tolerate the contradiction of their involvement in the war.

What, after all, was a black man doing in Vietnam fighting a yellow man for a white man who, historically, had sought to dominate all nonwhite peoples? For Abraham Blackman the weight of the contradiction is exacerbated through historical study, which reveals that blacks have always been treated like pawns after risking their lives in defense of this nation's interests.

After studying black military history and meeting with black veterans, Blackman is a complete man and a revolutionary. As a soldier in Korea he is content to dryly observe black soldiers "out-whiteying whitey" by coolly labeling Koreans "gooks." In Vietnam, after study and reflection, he will not let his troops behave this way: " 'No,' he thinks as he watches his men change. 'We're not joining in this shit. We ain't paying that price for belonging' " (Williams, 315). In addition to Blackman's active condemnation of black soldiers' tendency to dehumanize the enemy through racist stereotyping and therefore to feel good about barbaric acts is the more profound observation that for the black soldier to have a chance of belonging, not only must he lose his history but he must function as an imitation white soldier. Doing so means adopting and using whites' prejudices—even if those same prejudices are at times aimed at him. Blackman's newly acquired historical consciousness allows him to see that black soldiers have not benefited from previous attempts to imitate white soldiers.

His awareness of this historical cycle of black military history makes profound demands on Blackman. His study shows the black soldier repeatedly duped into service on the promise of everything from land to money to finally enjoying the full rights and privileges of the country for which he fights.

Through the course of the novel, Blackman moves from being a confused adolescent who limps into New York City to a self-assured revolutionary who brings America to her knees. The change occurs because external events force Blackman to consider black military history. The cultural-historical dimension of Blackman's movement helps us to understand why so many Afro-Americans fighting in Vietnam chose an array of symbolic responses to help themselves understand their involvement in the war and to ward off the effects of discrimination. Their cultural-historical demands are but less dramatic instances of what Blackman does through historical study and travel. In both instances, historical understanding is key to advancing the quest for freedom and literacy.

References

Anthony, F. C. " 'Pound,' A New Unity Sign; Ritual Greeting of Black Soldiers in Vietnam." *America* 124 (13 February 1971): 1478.
"Black Power in Vietnam." *Time*, 19 September 1969, pp. 22–23.
"Democracy in the Foxhole." *Time*, 26 May 1967, pp. 15–19.
DuBois, W.E.B. *The Souls of Black Folk*. 1903. Reprint. New York: New American Library, 1969.
Foner, Jack D. *Blacks and the Military in American History*. New York: Praeger, 1974.
Gibson, Donald B. *Five Black Writers: Essays on Wright, Ellison, Baldwin, Hughes and Leroi Jones*. New York: New York University Press, 1970.
"How Negroes Perform In Vietnam: With Chart." *U.S. News and World Report*, 15 August 1966, pp. 60–63.
Llorens, David. "Why Blacks Re-enlist." *Ebony*, August 1968, pp. 87–92.

Margolies, Edward. *Native Sons: A Critical Study of Twentieth Century Negro Authors*. Philadelphia: Lippincott, 1968.

Meier, August. *Negro Thought in America, 1880–1915*. Ann Arbor: University of Michigan Press, 1971.

Meier, August, Elliot Rudwick, and Francis L. Broderick. *Black Protest Thought in the Twentieth Century*. 2d ed. New York: Bobbs-Merrill, 1965.

Mullen, Robert W. *Blacks in America's Wars*. New York: Monad Press, 1973.

Snead, Gerald. "Vietnam: A Brother's Account." In *Vietnam and Black America*, edited by Clyde Taylor. Garden City, N.Y.: Doubleday, 1973. Pp. 223–42.

Terry, Wallace. *Bloods*. New York: Random House, 1984.

———. "Bringing the War Home." In *Vietnam and Black America*, edited by Clyde Taylor. Garden City, N.Y.: Doubleday, 1973. Pp. 200–219.

Williams, John A. *Captain Blackman*. Garden City, N.Y.: Doubleday, 1972.

3

Coming Home:
Ending Alienation

The central characters in George Davis's *Coming Home*, Ben and Childress, do not advance the quest for freedom and literacy in as clear and forceful a fashion as does Abraham Blackman in Williams's novel. Ben and Childress do move through the first two stages of meaning—happiness at the possibility of proving themselves men and disillusionment occasioned by racism—but by the end of the novel, they are just beginning a serious search for precedents in the racial memory that can help them understand their war experience.

Through the development of these two characters we see the way two forms of socialization worked to alienate the black Vietnam soldier from himself and from his history. The alienation results in both characters seeing the war in limited and individualized ways. Ben is the victim of bourgeois socialization buttressed by his Harvard education. Whereas intuition and instinct once might have gotten him through puzzling situations, now he is burdened with a plodding intellectualism that often renders him incapable of handling the questions his war experience thrusts upon him. Childress is the victim of a pedestrian form of socialization most frequently expressed through movies and television shows that champion the individual as conqueror or hero. Functioning at this level, he does not see a need to generalize his experience. Childress feels that the war is an opportunity to prove himself a man.

Both characters bring to Vietnam an assortment of preoccupations which the war serves to clarify. Ben's self-alienation is ended when he undergoes a kind of exorcism in which he casts off the bourgeois baggage of Harvard and goes AWOL. Childress finds the end of self-alienation in a prison cell. His inability to generalize the war experience makes it impossible for him to understand his own pain and confusion. The rage within him is eventually kindled, and Childress accidentally kills a policeman.

Coming Home provides a more personal look at the anguish and confusion of blacks who fought in Vietnam than does Williams's novel. Davis accomplishes this sense of intimacy with his characters through the movement of action and by allowing each of the novel's eleven characters to speak in the first person. These techniques combine to create an intricate mosaic that captures the war's broad influence as well as its effect on individuals.

The narrative moves from Thailand to Washington, D.C., back to Thailand, then to Schenectady, New York, back again to Washington, then to Thailand, and ends in Washington. The geographic movement illustrates the global influences of the war on people's lives. For example, an obscure thought by a character in Thailand is related to some action by a character in the United States. Stacy, one of the white characters in Thailand, and his girlfriend, who trudges along well-worn paths of American conservatism in Schenectady, New York, think about the difficulty they have in knowing black people: "I know there was something bothering him [he is thinking of Ben]. It started as soon as he got over here. His personality was always three quarters hidden" (Davis, 122). Roxanna ponders the same question and concludes, "You never know what they're thinking. You live on the same continent with them and you never know what they're thinking" (Davis, 98). The Vietnam War has the effect of shrinking the world because it is an event to which all the characters must respond.

The first-person narration allows us to see how both black and white characters piece together their lives under the pressure of a life-and-death situation, and it reveals motivations even they are not sure of: the reader knows the situations in which the characters operate and can consequently deduce their motivations based on what they say. As we listen to the white characters discuss everything from the affinity blacks and Asians have for each other to real-estate speculations, and then to black characters bemoan the unfairness and the contradictory nature of their situation, it becomes clear that black and white soldiers have very different views of the war. Thus although both face death and must learn to function under that stress, there are profound differences in the ways they cope with being in Vietnam.

The issue of socialization is crucial to understanding another dimension of the black soldier's experience in Vietnam. And here we turn first to Childress, for his development demonstrates how the war guaranteed a tragic end to his life. Childress serves as a metaphor for the numerous black Vietnam veterans who were unable to generalize their war experience and therefore ended in prison, addicted to drugs, or killed in civilian disputes.

Childress appears to be very sure of himself throughout the bulk of the novel, but by the end we find that he, like Ben, was searching for the meaning of his being in Vietnam. Childress is unable to move totally from the first level of meaning—the idea that service in the war will prove him a man. To be sure, he sees and discusses racist practices of white commanders and peers, but like the young Blackman he thinks that the dilemma of double-consciousness can be resolved by accomplishing tasks, that another act of heroism or another good deed will assure his acceptance by white America. He never learns that the dilemma of double-consciousness does not lend itself to static, onetime resolutions; that dilemma can be effectively handled only by viewing it as an ongoing aspect of life.

Early in the novel Childress thinks about leaving the war after flying his final mission: "For a moment I almost wish I'd see a Mig today so I could get me one before I go home. Win another medal. Take it back to Baltimore and wear it in the man's face. When he says: 'Boy' I'll say 'Boy my ass,' and slap him across his motherfuckin nose with one of my medals" (Davis, 13). Because any relationship between the "man" who conceives and directs the war effort and the "man" who might slip and call Childress "Boy" is not acknowledged, Childress can move with a straightforwardness based on ignorance. The ignorance that limits Childress results from his personalizing his involvement in the war and thereby failing to see that he is merely acting out a scripted role.

Childress's thinking on this subject reflects the thinking of some black Vietnam soldiers, particularly those who fought in elite units. Thomas H. Johnson, writing in 1968 about young black members of the elite 173d Airborne Brigade, explains how those soldiers viewed themselves: "Status, a proof of manhood and a youthful pursuit of excitement can be seen over and over again the aims of the teen aged young bloods" (Johnson, 32). These soldiers operated within the first level of meaning—a desire to prove themselves men—and consequently did not think critically about the war. Like Childress, their involvement was purely personal, and they projected consequences on a personal level. Johnson quotes one such soldier, " 'Man we kicked tail, much tail, on that hill' " (Johnson, 32). These young warriors, like Childress, believed their heroism would be rewarded. Of course, black soldiers have historically made such assumptions, and they have seldom been corroborated by the actions of whites after a war ends.

Another example of the tendency to personalize involvement in the war is illustrated by a black soldier's response to being asked if he would leave the service to participate in civil rights and black power demonstrations: " 'If I were to quit fighting and go home, people would hate the Negro more. But maybe a white man here writes home that a Negro saved his life. That eases the situation at home' " ("How Negroes Perform in Vietnam," 63). This soldier reduces a complex set of historical facts—racism and its use to exploit black soldiers during times of war—into a simple and personal equation which he assumes will have broad applicability. To be sure, individual whites no doubt raised their opinions of Afro-Americans as a result of the war. But such instances, though useful in a limited sense, do not address the entire question of institutional racism. During the early stages of the war, the Afro-American soldier generally ignored the broad issue of racism and viewed the possible results from a purely personal standpoint.

Childress's appearance of self-confidence is thus based on his inability to see himself as part of a larger scheme. As he flies his final mission he thinks about Damg, a Thai prostitute, and Ben: "I think about Ben and my moonfaced, yellow-brown whore who I risked court martial to take away from a stupid-assed white colonel. . . . Because she thought I was a confused and fucked up motherfucker like Ben. But I wanted her pussy, not her sympathy. 'Soul-brudder, soul-brudder. I'm same-same you,' she used to say. She came to me and she found I didn't need her love. I just wanted her to be with me. The finest whore south of Bangkok" (Davis, 15). Childress's need to assure himself that he is not confused and that he just wanted Damg to be with him is a clue that he has a problem. He attempts to reduce the political tone that Damg wants to place on their relationship to its simplest form, sexual conquest. Of course, if sexual conquest were the only basis for the relationship, anyone could have filled the bill. Damg is special partly because of her political perspective, and this specialness is illustrated in two additional ways. First, Childress risks court-martial by "stealing" Damg from a white officer; second, when he leaves the service, he cannot accept the possibility of Damg being with Ben. These are not the concerns of a man who simply wants "pussy."

To keep Ben and Damg apart, Childress plants communist material in Damg's room and alerts the authorities. Because Damg and Ben are seeing each other, Ben is implicated as a possible communist sympathizer. Functionally this makes no difference because Ben goes AWOL before the material is found. Childress's actions, however, demonstrate his need for self-understanding and the ability to place himself within a historical context. His failure to reach an understanding concerning these issues while he is in the military results in problems once he leaves the service. The rage that results from the contradictory nature of his Vietnam involvement leads him to spontaneous acts of violence that he cannot fully understand.

From a jail cell in Baltimore, Childress explains to Rose, Ben's wife, that he planted the communist material in Damg's room. Rose is trying to gather information that will lessen the trouble Ben is in for going AWOL and for having communist material in his possession: " 'It was my stuff. I used to read stuff like that. I got it in Hong Kong.' " I look at Rose. " 'I explained all that. Rose, I was looking for answers too, just like everyone else. Everyone thought I knew all the answers, because I seemed so sure of myself, but I was searching like a lot of other people. That part is true Rose' " (Davis, 185). Ironically, Childress's self- assured projection of himself made it difficult for him to interact with other Afro-American soldiers who were also searching for meaning. In Vietnam, racial fraternization was a prerequisite for the Afro-American soldier to be politicized, but for the "tough guy" loner who moved through the war like a remorseless mercenary, there was little chance for such fraternization. Cut off from a community, Childress has difficulty discovering himself in the context of racial history. Again he attempts to explain exactly why he ended up in jail:

"I don't know. I was walking down the street in Baltimore in the middle of the day and this young black dude was handing out leaflets on the corner. So I took one and started to read it. Then this big ugly cop come up and told me to get moving like that. So I told him to wait a minute until I finish reading my little leaflet. And he said, 'Get your black ass moving. *Now.*' I said, 'Man, I got a Constitutional right to be here just like everybody else.' 'This is all the Constitution you need.' So I go to get in my car, and when I started to get in, the cracker kicked me dead in the ass. So, I picked up a jack handle and knocked the gun out of his hand and knocked him down. He killed his own damn self when his head hit the concrete. All I was trying to do was teach him not to kick anybody any more. I tried to tear his leg off." (Davis, 185–86)

In a sense, Childress's actions are inevitable. The failure to harmonize the desire to be a hero with his knowledge of racism creates a tension that has to be resolved. Striking the policeman helps to resolve that tension. His failure to move beyond the personal level made it inevitable that he would react to any provocation in a highly spontaneous and personal manner. It is unlikely, for example, that Abraham Blackman would have been pulled into the confrontation with the white policeman; Blackman has a grand plan that goes beyond responding to specific acts of racism.

In the context of the returning veteran, Childress's actions are understandable. After all, he risked his life to defend rights he does not enjoy as a citizen of the country for which he fought. One of the clearest statements on this dilemma comes from Frank Peterson, an Afro-American soldier who fought in Vietnam: " 'The average black who has been here and goes back to the States is bordering somewhere on the psychotic as a result of having grown up a black man in America—having been given this black pride and then going back to find that nothing has changed' " ("Black Power in Vietnam," 23). Though Childress is not psychotic, it is clear that he has numerous problems with the tensions created by functioning between the first two levels of meaning. His striking the policeman is as understandable as it is inevitable.

A more dramatic instance of a black soldier's inability to deal with the contradiction of risking his life and then experiencing racism in the country for which he took those risks is that of Mark Essex, a Vietnam veteran who killed several whites at a New Orleans Howard Johnson's in 1973. *Time* magazine describes the event:

A besieging army of 200 uniformed sharpshooters and volunteers surrounded the motel. As the cordon tightened, the assailants found refuge behind the concrete walls of the rooftop's boiler room and stairwell casements. An armor-plated Marine helicopter made repeated passes as the cops tried to blast through the walls, but the sniper shots kept coming. Finally, eleven hours after the violence had begun, one lone sniper darted under the glare of a helicopter spotlight, ran about 30 ft. in a zigzag pattern across the roof top and fell dead in a hail of police tracer bullets, his body riddled with more than 100 slugs. ("Death in New Orleans," 20)

It took the police more than ten hours to decide that Essex had acted alone. When they investigated his past, they were dumbfounded. One police officer noted that Essex was the best trainee in the city's vocational classes for the "hard-core unemployed." The irony of this veteran being among the "hard-core unemployed" did not register with the officer or with others who commented on his case.

Essex's reasons for his actions were much like those of Childress in that he was unable to generalize his plight through historical study or cultural search. Indeed, like Childress, Essex was a loner and therefore limited in experiencing the racial fraternization which is so necessary in fiction and in the world for characters and individuals to handle their predicaments successfully. Essex went AWOL and was court-martialed. He testified at his hearing: " 'I had begun to hate all white people. I was tired of going to white people and telling them my problems and not getting anything done about it.' " His mother explained: " 'It all started in the Navy. He was all right when he left here [home].' " She concluded, " 'I do think [Mark] was driven to this. . . . Jimmy [Mark] was trying to make white America stand up and be aware of what is happening to us' " ("Death in New Orleans," 21). Confronted at every turn by the contradictory nature of the black military man's existence in America, the young Mark Essex sought to alleviate the psychological tension resulting from that contradiction.

Essex was unable to find a nonviolent way of dealing with this contradiction. Rather, like the fictional Abraham Blackman, he chose to strike at America's domestic military, the police (four of the six whites he killed were policemen). The almost noble desperation of his actions is as allegorical as are the actions of Abraham Blackman in that both stem from the need to alter the power relationships between blacks and whites, which are projected allegorically as the fundamental cause of double-consciousness. The case of Mark Essex provides a striking example of the tragedy of black Vietnam era veterans who are not able to find a nonviolent way to deal with the tensions caused by racism.

The examples of Childress and Essex also illustrate what happens when the Afro-American soldier individualizes his tour of duty in Vietnam. The difficulty such soldiers have in advancing the quest for freedom and literacy is reflected in their actions after leaving the service.

Ben's situation is quite different. Within the realm of bourgeois socialization, four events alienate him from himself and his history: his experience at Harvard, his marriage to Rose, his tour of duty in Vietnam, and his decision to go AWOL. Though Ben never fully reaches the third stage of development (clear historical understanding and action), as the novel ends he is less divided than he initially was. An analysis of these four events will help us to understand Vietnam era Afro-American soldiers whose alienation from themselves and from their history led them to go AWOL.

Ben is a Harvard graduate and suffers from a mixture of self-alienation and guilt as a result of the privilege of having that opportunity. He dramatically severs his racial roots as a result of his Harvard experience. Harvard here functions to rid the infidel of superstition and all modes of knowing that spring from intuitive paradigms. The following quote illustrates this loss: "In some places the air is chilly, and in others it is warm. Walking through ghosts, we used to say before everything became literal and scientific, and then became more unreal than it was before, leading straight to Vietnam. Before a million explanations came down on me and what I wanted to feel and then all the explanations proved to be lies" (Davis, 27–28). Beyond the need to return to an intuitive way of knowing the world that is not scientifically demonstrable is a subtle desire to be a part of an Afro-American continuum that simultaneously precedes and goes beyond the specific stimulus—walking through warm air—that sparked Ben's musing. The continuum he seeks is superficially folk in appearance, an unschooled explanation of a physical phenomenon: atmospheric changes result from the presence of spirits. Such explanations are outside the realm of scientific verifiability, and in addition there is the Western prejudice against metaphysics. Thus it is understandable that Ben's education at one of America's most prestigious centers of cultural dissemination should move him away from African and Afro-American traditions. But for Afro-Americans, metaphysics is one projection of spirituality, and spirituality, in one form or another, has always permeated the day-to-day activities of Afro-Americans. Thus Ben's seemingly casual reflection about walking through ghosts is an attempt to get back to a way of perceiving reality that is continuous with his past. The reflection is a cerebral casting into a historical sea: he is looking for solid ground, a reference point from which to launch clear forays into self- and racial understanding.

Ben's desire to resurrect an aspect of his personal history is similar to ways that other black soldiers in the world sought to make sense of their Vietnam War involvement. A reporter has written, "The standard greeting [among black soldiers] includes two taps on the chest—meaning 'I will die for you.' In 'Soul Alley,' some blacks add a swift downward motion of the hand—a stroke to kill" ("Soul Alley," 40). This particular form of the soul handshake was current among black soldiers in 1970, a time when blacks were extremely aggrieved over being discriminated against by whites. The times dictated that an old expression of greeting assume new meanings, which were intended to assure psychological peace and, in some cases, physical safety from whites through group solidarity. The soul handshake and other symbolic methods of greeting that black soldiers used were merely attempts to establish the psychological space necessary to make the war experience understandable and manageable. These soldiers' actions were drawn from the racial past, and, like Ben's reflections concerning walking through ghosts, they were attempts to obtain literacy.

The malaise that Ben experiences as a result of his Harvard education prepares him for his stay in Vietnam. He transplants the bundle of contradictions that Harvard helped create to an alien shore. Before looking at the changes Harvard induced in Ben, however, a look at his marital life is instructive. For it too is without singular focus and consequently contributes to the confusion that he brings with him to Vietnam.

Rose reflects on her failure to give Ben what he needed: "Ben married me because he had to learn again what it meant to be black after four years of Harvard. I should have helped him with that" (Davis, 36). Although we are not given much information about Rose's past, one can gather that she belongs to that class of blacks who through some odd confluence of media hype and parental guidance or nonguidance are socialized to believe in America's symbols and icons even when individual and racial experience contradicts those symbols and icons. She is determined to emulate the values and actions of the wives of the white officers at the base where they are stationed. As a consequence, Rose further complicates Ben's desire to recapture elements of his personal history that, because of their Afro-Americanness, could provide an end to the confusion Harvard and the military create.

Rose wants to perform middle-class masquerades in response to stimuli from the whites on the base. She reflects: "Ben said I hated him because he wouldn't play husbandsey-wifesey games like the white people on television and on the base do. I wanted to be the little woman, the modern American housewife with the little apron and all. The great little housekeeper with French Provincial furniture to dust every day while I waited for hubby. Ben wouldn't cooperate so when he wanted me to be the first officer's wife in the Air Force to get an Afro I went to the beauty parlor and got it straightened as slick as they could make it, and dyed it red, like a fool" (Davis, 36–37). This couple has special problems that are not representative of those faced by the majority of black couples affected by the war. As a pilot, an officer, and a Harvard graduate, Ben, and by extension his wife, have more options available to them than did the majority of Afro-Americans involved in the war. Rose's actions help us understand a middle-class trait that causes some black women to fail to meet the needs of male friends, lovers, and husbands who desire a historically conscious existence. This middle-class trait is to see racial amnesia as necessary to the singular march into the melting pot. But Rose is at least capable of reflection. When Ben went "to the nam" she got "the biggest, bushiest damn Afro you ever saw." Realizing the foolishness of the entire episode—first dying her hair red and later getting an Afro—she concludes, " 'Shit, I feel like spitting in my own face' " (Davis, 37).

Rose is among the characters indirectly affected by the war, and she needs to be in Vietnam or to have to deal more directly with the consequences of the war if she is to get beyond the constraints her socialization has placed upon her. To be racially conscious, she must exorcise the American Dream. Only then, armed with a historical perspective, can she sift through the contradiction of the American experience and decide what aspects of it are useful to self-understanding.

Ben's refusal to play Ozzie to Rose's Harriet is an attempt to break free of stereotypical roles that a young black officer and his wife are expected to play. Similarly, his desire for Rose to wear her hair in an Afro at the ball is more than a wish that his wife look fashionable: he wants her appearance to be consistent with his notion of how a black woman should look. But Ben's refusal to play "husbandsey-wifesey games" as well as his demand that she wear an Afro are undercut by the fact that he could have avoided going into the Air Force altogether. "A Harvard man doesn't have to come into the war. There are ways of getting out of it. But how could I have escaped the fate of the oppressed without using the privilege of the oppressor?" (Davis, 110). Even if Ben had chosen differently—perhaps graduate school or accepting a job in education, government, or the private sector—he still would have made a choice within the context of the privileges earned in four years at Harvard. So the issue is not so much whether or not he went to Vietnam as it is harmonizing his Harvard experience with his earlier black self. Rose does not help him with this problem because she has not moved beyond delimiting forms of socialization. So when Ben lands in Vietnam, he has no direction-giving precedents from experiences shared with his wife. To deal with his loneliness, his inability to communicate, and his incessant introspection, he must look to other areas of his personal history and certainly to the panoply of precedents in his racial past.

Vietnam only exacerbates these problems, and to resolve them he must alter either the way he thinks or his involvement in the war. During the period when he is unable to do either, he lapses into disillusionment. The changes Ben undergoes are similar to those experienced by many Afro-Americans. In both instances the individual has to harmonize the contradictory nature of his involvement. Jay Wright, a black man who ultimately deserted, explains his decision: " 'I was sitting at my desk back in Louisiana, looking at 752's take off and land. I realized that we were bombing women and children and I also remembered what I had seen over there [Vietnam]—much racial hatred against the Vietnamese people on the part of the white soldiers. I felt that here in Sweden I could speak out against the injustices committed against my people' " (Nilson, 122). To make sense of his life, Wright had either to forget what he knew about America and American involvement in Vietnam or leave the military. Unless he made one of these decisions, he was destined to a life of tension and self-alienation. He chose to defect to Sweden. Wright's situation is not unique among Afro-American soldiers who reflected on the meaning of the war in the context of Afro-American military history. Don Williams states emphatically: " 'To us, the fight is not over once there is peace in Vietnam. The main reason—and I can not stress this enough—for my own defection is the injustices committed against my people in the U.S. I will not rest until their awful conditions have been changed' " (Nilson, 122).

For Ben, the contradiction between what he sees and what he feels results in a baseless suspicion of the Thai people and an inability to communicate. A Thai woman is busy cleaning his room: "I would like to joke and talk with her, but I always hesitate because I don't know what these people think of me" (Davis, 86). Ben goes on to say that Harvard planted the seed of suspicion in his character, and this feeling is intensified because Childress gets along well with the Thai people: "He joked with them a lot. When he found out that most Thai people never have tasted apples, he ordered a bushel of apples from the commissary and passed them out among the girls. He knows how to make them laugh" (Davis, 85).

When Ben decides that he will fly no future missions, much of the confusion that characterizes his life evaporates. His relationship with the Thai people is no longer problematic. Ben relates his decision not to fly to Stacy, a white pilot with whom he shares a bunk:

> [Ben] "I came back with a full load of bombs. . . . I told them they wouldn't toggle and they wouldn't jettison."
> [Stacy] "They didn't believe you."
> [Ben] "I guess not. . . ."
> [Stacy] "They think you just didn't want to drop them."
> [Ben] "They're right. I didn't see any troop concentration. It looked like a village. I couldn't drop them. Stacy I decided what I am going to do. When I get back from Bangkok, I'm not going to fly anymore. I'm tired of helping white men keep their hold over the world." (Davis, 88)

Ben's trip to Bangkok is enjoyable because he has moved the poles of his personality closer together. He says that he is "no longer anxious about what the Thai people might think about Negroes." When he is

on a boat ride with Damg while still in Bangkok, the Thai fisherman
who captains their boat speaks pleasantly to Damg in Thai. She tells
Ben, " 'Thai people like you. . . . He say you same-same Thai
people.' "

Ben and Damg visit a bar filled with black enlisted men. The
Thai band is known as " 'Big Buddha and his' the other words are
hidden by a trumpet case." Ben is moved by Big Buddha's rendition
of Wilson Pickett's "I Found a Love": " 'Go 'head Big Buddha. . . .
Go 'head with yo bad self.' " A Black GI near me laughs. 'Buddha is
into his shit ain't he?' 'If Big Buddha does a James Brown, I'm gonna
fall out,' the GI says. 'Shit! You? Me. They gon' have to carry me out.'
'I know what you mean' " (Davis, 139). The bantering connects to a
time when Ben was not divided and was more free.

Ben later visits the African Star, a bar "owned by three black ex-
GI's who got out of the Army and stayed in Bangkok." The bar
reminds Ben of the Hollywood Club in Washington, D.C., a place he
frequented while stationed at Andrews Air Force Base. Ben meets a
black enlisted man who is AWOL and preparing to seek asylum in
Sweden. Their conversation results in Ben's deciding not to return to
his unit after he leaves Bangkok. The soldier explains the events
leading up to his decision to seek asylum:

> "The night before I left the 'Nam I was on patrol in a village near Thuc Yen
> and this little kid came up to me in an alley and asked me did I want a shoe
> shine. And sometimes they have bombs in those boxes. So I told him to set
> his box down and back off, and he turned and ran and I shot him right in the
> back. . . . Then I went up and looked in his little box and do you know what
> I found? Shoe polish man. Not a goddamn thing but shoe polish. I went back
> to the base and packed my shit. I ain't never gon kill no more innocent
> people. . . . And I ain't going to no jail either." (Davis, 169)

Ben wishes the soldier well and then considers "all the black
men who have been hitting the road, catching trains." Ben then
thinks about "all the black men in prison or in southern prison farms"
and tries to compare the two groups. For Ben, "hitting the road" or
"catching trains" symbolizes a characteristic black response to impossible situations. In the context of this tradition, Ben's decision to
desert is less the act of an individual motivated by anger and frustration than that of a man conscious of the ways his ancestors responded
to like circumstances. In this sense, Ben is reminiscent of the slaves

who chose attempted escape to the certainty of continued oppression, or, indeed, to the thousands of blacks who, during the first part of this century, chose the promise of a better life up north to the certainty of hard times in the South.

Ben's dilemma is not unique to the black pilot or officer. Many black veterans felt that even if their lives took bizarre turns as a result of their decision to seek asylum, that choice was preferable to continued involvement in the war. Many of these soldiers bemoaned the problems resulting from that decision, but almost to a man, they were glad they had done it. As one said, " 'I don't want to go back to the states and certainly not back to Houston, Texas. . . . They would call me a nigger and my wife a gook' " ("Soul Alley," 40). Other soldiers regretted not being able to see members of their families but remained steadfast in their desire to remain in Sweden.

After the conversation in the bar, Ben tramps back to the hotel room that he shares with Damg, leaves her money and a note, and begins to move toward seeking political asylum in Sweden. We are not told what happens to him, and this omission is understandable. For the most striking element in his experience is a process that we see in the other novels discussed in this section and in the accounts of actual Vietnam War soldiers: for a character or a real individual to attain psychological peace he must stop viewing his experience in purely individual terms and somehow relate to relevant dimensions of black world history. Ben makes that connection with a tradition of calculated desperation that places a premium on preserving integrity: a negative situation must be altered even if the results are fraught with uncertainty. Ben's early reflection about walking through ghosts and how Harvard undermined his folkways signifies the beginning of this process. When he stops flying bombing missions and goes AWOL the process is complete. The psychological peace he attains results in a clear condemnation of the war:

> I wonder why there could not be some kind of divine law that says man can only come to another man's country as a tourist, not as colonizers or exploiters. But when white men came to countries where people were just sitting on natural resources—just living and having babies and trying to be happy—they called them lazy and backward or uncivilized. They hated them and justified whatever they did to them by invoking some kind of divine right of commerce. Discovered them, christianized them, annihilated them

or turned them into tools—hoes and cotton pickers and brooms and shoe-shine boys—for the great march of civilization. (Davis, 119)

This condemnation is free of self-doubt and self-recrimination.

Despite the war's overall negative effect on most characters, for Ben, ironically, it serves a positive function. It forces him to harmonize the two selves that Harvard created, and this allows him to appropriate an aspect of his racial past that helps him deal with the situation at hand.

It is common for young men to mature and work out problems while in the military, but what is significant here is that for black soldiers maturity often means moving away from the country for which they ostensibly are fighting. Depending on a range of variables, the move may be physical, as with Ben, or it may be psychological, as we will see among characters and individuals to be discussed in the next chapter.

References

"Black Power in Vietnam." *Time*, 19 September 1969, pp. 22–23.

Davis, George. *Coming Home*. New York: Random House, 1971.

"Death in New Orleans." *Time*, 22 January 1973, pp. 20–21.

Gwaltney, John Langston, comp. *Drylongso: A Self-Portrait of Black America*. New York: Random House, 1980.

"How Negroes Perform in Vietnam: With Chart." *U.S. News and World Report*, 15 August 1966, pp. 60–63.

Johnson, Thomas H. "Negroes in the Nam." *Ebony*, August 1968, pp. 32–36.

Levine, Laurence. *Black Culture and Black Consciousness: Afro-American Folk Thought from Slavery to Freedom*. New York: Oxford University Press, 1977.

Nilson, Ulf. "Deserters in Sweden." *Ebony*, August 1968, pp. 120–22.

"Soul Alley, Home for Black AWOLs and Deserters." *Time*, 14 December 1970, pp. 39–40.

4

Tragic Magic:
A Metaphorical Solution

Wesley Brown's *Tragic Magic* traces the development of two central characters, Otis and Ellington, who are shaped by the events of Vietnam, the civil rights movement, and the black power movement. Again, socialization is key to understanding the inability of one of the characters to deal with his post-Vietnam experience. In Otis we see the alienating effects of American socialization on a young black who joins the army to fight in Vietnam in hopes of achieving the ideal he has been taught to believe in. In this sense, Otis is similar to the young Captain Blackman, Childress in Davis's novel, and individuals in the real world such as Mark Essex. In each instance, the man is unable to discover a tradition in the racial memory that will allow him to adjust to and move beyond the limitations created by the war experience. Melvin Ellington is not the victim of socialization in the same way that makes it impossible for Otis to deal with life after Vietnam. Through Ellington's various political involvements he moves from adolescence to become a self-accepting man who may or may not engage in revolutionary activity. He discovers a historically conscious way to live that does not violate his personality. In this sense, Ellington is most like Ben in *Coming Home* in that internal peace is more important to him than making an attempt to change the power relationships between blacks and whites.

Brown's use of jazz aesthetics as a narrative referent influences language and the conceptualization of ideas in the novel and also provides an obvious perspective for viewing and predicting the ways characters confront and deal with problems. His jazz aesthetic is similar to my use of the terms *freedom* and *literacy* in that it emphasizes the personalized expression of racial knowledge. Those characters who are able to appropriate the aesthetic do well and can solve problems. They advance the quest for freedom and literacy. Those who are unable to appropriate the aesthetic remain trapped in frenetic activity which they do not fully understand. They do not advance the quest for freedom and literacy.

Jazz aesthetics consists of technical knowledge of one's instrument, knowledge of one's own idiosyncrasies which can be understood as a personal style, and knowledge of one's audience. Scatting is the language of Brown's jazz aesthetic, and he defines *scatology* as "a branch of science dealing with the diagnosis of dung and other excremental matters of state. Talking shit is a renegade form of scatology developed by people who were fed up with do-do dialogues and created a kind of vocal doodling that suggested other possibilities within the human voice beyond the same old shit" (Brown, 5).

When characters can devise their own "arrangements" they have begun the process of advancing the quest for freedom and literacy. The ability to devise arrangements is an indication not only of being able to "scat" but, more important, is a realization of the emotional and rational components of the jazz aesthetic. From an emotional standpoint, jazz aesthetics are incantation, a manifestation of sounds that alters reality in pre- or extralogical ways. When the musical metaphor is applied to life, the result is a verbal dexterity that allows characters or individuals in the real world to alter situations through their control of words. The rational component of jazz aesthetics directs informed practitioners to the proper time and place for expression. Because in the traditional sense, there are no correct preexistent times or places, "scatting" avoids a careful relativism by placing itself on a level not fully accessible by either logic or emotion. In discovering and expressing his own mix of logic and emotion, the individual practitioner finds his own voice.

The process that leads to finding one's voice is similar in function to the process of racial fraternization that was so crucial in Blackman's development and in Ben's decision to go AWOL. In both instances, individuals adopt an outlook that allows them to generalize their experience so they can distinguish peril from opportunity.

This outlook guides them to actions that assure self-preservation, thereby providing a basis for future advancement.

Ellington is able to devise his own arrangements, but Otis is not. Nor is there much evidence in the novel to suggest that fraternization was part of Otis's Vietnam experience. Indeed, his attempt to live the ideal in which he has been socialized to believe creates a layer of abstraction that might well impede his recognition of the mutuality of experience involved in fraternization. Otis's socialization also prevents him from discovering traditions within Afro-American history. Otis, unlike Ellington, never learns that important dimensions of the Afro-American future lie in creative-cultural expressions of the Afro-American past.

Otis is not able to take advantage of any particular Afro-American tradition, and as a result he is never able to move out from under the shadow of his Vietnam experience. His major problem is an inability to square his preconceived notion of Vietnam with the reality of his war experience, for the socialization to which he is subjected is completely at odds with his personal and racial history.

Otis explains a recurring dream he has about John Wayne. The "Duke" is distraught at being declared unfit for the armed services—he has bad knees. Determined not to let this situation preclude heroics, Wayne storms Alcatraz during an Indian occupation, and for his trouble he is caught and sentenced to the Pacific Ocean: "While he is treading water, Woody Strode, the black cat in *Sergeant Rutledge,* paddles by in a canoe singing the blues: 'everybody wants to go to heaven / but nobody wants to die / Everybody wants to know the reason / but never get past the why" (Brown, 98). The blues lyrics in the dream allude to the contradiction between a desired goal and the actions necessary to achieve that goal. Here the hero wants accolades but is not willing to take the risks the nameless stuntman routinely takes. In a metaphoric sense, John Wayne's stuntman is undoubtedly black—the front man in Vietnam who suffers the highest casualty rates but does not receive the praise his actions demand.

To be sure, during the early stages of the war the black soldier did have praises heaped on him by blacks and whites. But as the war escalated, the focus in black America shifted from praise to worry, for the black soldier was no longer interested in proving himself, and no wonder: his casualty rates were always greater than the percentage of his military involvement. Additionally, a disproportionate number of black soldiers ended up in stockades and brigs, "where besides outworn facilities and severe overcrowding, food was poor and rations short, sanitation was defective and inhumane treatment was rampant" (Foner, 209). So, in questioning black unrest, the military authorities never got past the why: they could not see a connection between a desired goal (loyal and obedient Afro-American soldiers) and the treatment necessary to obtain that goal. And the deeper contradictions of the war made it impossible for the military to rely indefinitely on black soldiers. Before a large number of black soldiers became militant, the authorities assumed they could exact loyalty and obedience without recognizing the uniqueness of the black solider.

Otis does not interpret the dream as I do, but he is clear about why he is in Vietnam: " 'I sure believed all that war crap we used to see in the movies' " (Brown, 96). We see the tension between Otis's need to separate his experience in Vietnam from the heroics of Wayne's cinematic world and, paradoxically, even though he has lost a hand while fighting in Vietnam, to believe what his experience contradicts: " 'You know when I was in the Nam there was a village called Ben Suc that was rumored to be sympathetic to the V.C. But army intelligence was never able to prove it. So they finally ordered the destruction of the village. Those flicks did to my mind what them bulldozers did to Ben Suc. The funny thing is, I can't stop watching them. There's something in me that still wants to believe that the war was like what we used to see in the movies' " (Brown, 138). His desire to believe in the celluloid projections of Hollywood suggests that his path to self-realization through the traditional means of education and career was limited. Otis goes from high school to the army without investigating other avenues. Many blacks did go to colleges and universities, but it was not until 1968 that educational policies were challenged to increase the number of black students and faculty members at predominantly white educational institutions (Berry and Blassingame, 279–92).

In 1966 the military exploited the limited educational and career options available to young blacks by inaugurating Project 100,000, a program to induct and train men who had previously been rejected because of low educational scores. Most of the draftees were black and were never trained to do anything of use in a peacetime economy. Military officials later acknowledged that the program was a ruse to enlarge the pool of eligible draftees. The majority of the black troops fighting in Vietnam were not in Project 100,000, but they too were unable to use skills they learned there in a peacetime economy. Foner writes: "A serviceman looked to his military training to help him find employment after discharge. Most black servicemen found their training in combat specialties totally inapplicable to civilian life, leaving them with small chance of securing any job, let alone a well-paid one" (Foner, 209). The only option made available for undereducated and unskilled blacks during this period was the military. The propaganda mill simultaneously fed on and manipulated this limited opportunity to attract and keep black soldiers in Vietnam. The high reenlistment rates among black soldiers and their volunteering for hazardous duty are a function of the military propaganda. This propaganda also made some black soldiers want to prove themselves men.

While pursuing a manhood made unobtainable because of a reliance on the hostile external criteria of whites, a black soldier does not consider or reflect upon his personal and racial history. They are suspended. In Otis's case, this suspension ceases when he returns stateside. Through a job at a broadcasting studio he learns of an archive that contains all of John Wayne's films. Hoping to end his love-hate relationship with Wayne, Otis convinces his friend Melvin Ellington that it is safe to sneak into the archive and watch these films. Engrossed as a participant-observer in each film, Otis does not notice when the projector malfunctions, causing mounds of film to pile up. When Ellington turns on the lights, Otis snaps:

> "What the fuck you lookin't at?"
> "What do you mean?"
> "You think I've flipped out don't you?"
> "No, I don't think that."
> "Yes you do motherfucker. I ain't stupid. Just cause you didn't go in the service you think you better than me."
> "That's not true, Otis."
> "You callin' me a liar, motherfucker?" (Brown, 139)

Otis slams Ellington into the wall, setting off an alarm. They manage to escape after Ellington relates a fabrication—an example of verbal dexterity—to two policemen who stop them.

For Otis the reprieve is temporary. Because he is unable to

distinguish between what is real and what is not, he cannot formulate the question of a critical evaluation of his own history in a fashion that can be answered. What might be for many young black men a normal period of fascination with the theatrics of movie heroes becomes for Otis a self-denying reason for being that must end tragically.

For reasons not as starkly obvious as those of Otis, black soldiers whose socialization limited their perspectives were unable to square the ideal with the actual. The key characteristic that these soldiers share with Otis, however, is a lack of self-conscious historical perspective. For these men, everything that happened to them seemed the first such occurrence in history, and they therefore lacked the firm foundation that precedent provides. They were faced individually with the task of creating themselves.

A tragic example of a soldier awash in confusion occasioned by a war experience for which his personal history had not prepared him, either directly through experience or indirectly through historical study, is Dwight Johnson, a black Detroiter who won the Congressional Medal of Honor in 1968. Objectively the medal transformed Johnson from an unemployed and largely unemployable Vietnam veteran (one of his friends pointed out that Johnson often mumbled answers to questions asked during job interviews and generally behaved in a fashion that suggested he "felt inferior") to a high-salaried military recruiter to whom credit and other amenities were extended by Detroit area merchants. The award did not take away the insecurity that resulted from or was exacerbated by the war experience and that affected his job interviews (Nordheimer).

Several of Johnson's friends noted the changes in him caused by the war. His cousin said: " 'The thing that bugged me about Skip [Johnson] and the one thing that I thought was kind of strange and unlike him, was the pictures he brought back. He had a stack of dead people, you know, dead Vietnamese. Color slides.' " Another of Johnson's friends noted ways he was similar to other black Vietnam veterans: " 'It's like they don't have too much to say about what it was like over there. Maybe it's because they have killed people and they don't know why they killed them' " (Nordheimer, 234). This observation suggests a reason for the self-alienation that many black Vietnam veterans felt. To function in Vietnam required a disengagement from conscious moral guidelines concerning the taking of human life. Once this disengagement occurs, all soldiers, but particularly black soldiers, must find guidelines to replace the ones their actions have voided. The black soldier who is able to adopt a set of guidelines from some aspect of Afro-American history is able to quash self-alienation and be whole again. Johnson did not have that experience.

Johnson's unwillingness to talk about the war experience and his slides of dead Vietnamese may have been magnified by receipt of the Congressional Medal of Honor because the life it opened for him— speaking engagements and luncheons with Chamber of Commerce members intent on turning the hero into a commodity—was as foreign to him as Vietnam. Instead of a post-Vietnam period geared toward finding his roots, Johnson was futher alienated from those roots.

Johnson's specific act of heroism is useful in understanding his eventual death in a Detroit area suburb. A tank patrol of which he was a member until the previous night was destroyed, and when he saw his friends, black and white, incinerating he went berserk. Dodging bullets, Johnson ran from his tank to the one on fire and pulled a friend from the flames. The friend eventually died. Johnson then systematically hunted and killed twenty North Vietnamese. He was out of the service for several months before receiving the medal (Nordheimer, 235). He was not prepared to deal with the publicity and the expectations of him after he received the award. He talked less. Childhood stomach problems recurred and grew worse. He went to the army hospital, which eventually sent him to the psychiatric unit. The psychiatric report read, "Depression caused by post-Vietnam adjustment problems. In general, there is evidence the subject learned to live up to the expectations of others while there was a buildup of anger he continuously suppressed" (Nordheimer, 240–41).

The expectations that Johnson learned to live up to were based on the conglomeration of ideals that this country promulgates, essentially a belief in justice. The fictional Otis similarly adheres to ideals, but those he chooses involve the "leatherneck" marine liberating the infidel from himself, making him a willing host for democracy and justice.

Johnson asked the psychiatrist, "What would happen if I lost control of myself in Detroit and behaved like I did in Vietnam?" (Nordheimer, 245). Eventually Johnson, like Otis, put himself in a position to be killed. After losing his money by not handling it responsibly, he went to a Detroit suburb and tried to rob a store. The store owner reported: "I first hit him with two bullets. But he just stood there with the gun in his hand and said, 'I'm going to kill you.' " About the Vietnam episode that earned him the Congressional Medal of Honor, his psychiatrist reported: "The subject remembered coming face to face with a Vietnamese with a gun. He can remember the soldier squeezing the trigger. The gun jammed. The subject has since engaged in some magical thinking about the episode" (Nordheimer, 242–43).

For Otis, the fictional character in *Tragic Magic,* the inability to reconcile his war experience with the beliefs movies socialized him to hold drives him to put himself in a position to be killed. It is as though the certainty of death is preferable to a confused and apparently aimless existence. Though the specific dimensions of the socialization that shaped Johnson's thinking about the war experience are less clear than is the case for Otis, it is clear that Johnson was not prepared to deal with the contradictions his Vietnam and post-Vietnam experience generated. We do know that Johnson idealized a jammed gun into a myth of invincibility, and that myth was interpenetrated with guilt for not having died with his friends. Thus he set himself up to be killed.

In both the fictional and the real-life instances, the inability of individuals to see themselves within historical context ultimately makes their ends inevitable. The limited options available to an isolated individual are no match for the engulfing war experience.

Melvin Ellington's maturation beyond the early influences of his childhood hero, Otis, moves through three phases once he enters a New York City university. He is first an integrationist who attends "freedom highs" intended to help whites move beyond the narrow dimensions of racism. This liberation was a prerequisite to the political role of enlightened supporters of southern civil rights activity. Ellington next becomes a nationalist as a member of a group known as the Blue Monks. They answer all questions posed by whites with names of compositions written by Theolonius Monk. And finally he joins the "No Vietnamese Ever Called Me a Nigger Caucus." He takes the rhetoric of this group seriously, burns his draft card, refuses to be inducted into the service, and, as a result, goes to prison. In each of these moves Ellington is semiconscious; his failure to place his involvement in groups he joins in a self-conscious context makes the faddish and insecure individual appear sincere. Thus young Ellington is pulled into the integrationist politics of Theodore Sutherland, a black man, and Keith McDermott, Sutherland's white alter ago.

Ellington's desire to discover himself in the activist arena is an attempt to harmonize his personality with the political theories of integrationism, black power nationalism, and a nihilism derived from his antiwar activity. It is difficult for any activist to discover himself in the context of "revolutionary" activity when he has not come to a basic understanding about his personality. Without this knowledge, the activist may well discover that the consequences of his activism are in conflict with some aspect of his personality. No one involved in revolutionary action can always predict the consequences of that action, but those individuals who are comfortable with themselves and who know their strengths and weaknesses can adjust to changes more readily than those who do not know themselves. This dynamic may be viewed as a sudden revelation, an unplanned discovery of personal strengths and weaknesses.

This dynamic of personal discovery is evident in some early civil rights politics of the sixties. Robert Moses, a member of the Student Non-Violent Coordinating Committee, "became so worried that he might become another Martin Luther King, that he changed his name to Robert Parris and moved from Mississippi to Alabama in a conscious effort to battle the effects of his own charisma" (Sellers, 138). Cleve Sellers, also a SNCC member, tells about learning of Moses's name change:

> "I have a message for you," he [Moses] said. Everyone was immediately quiet. "I have changed my name. I will no longer be known as Robert Moses. From now on it will be Robert Parris. My wife's name is no longer Donna Richards." [Her maiden name is Richards.] . . . We thought he was finished. Some of those present began to clap. They stopped abruptly when he produced a bottle of wine and a large cut of cheese.
> "I want you to eat and drink," he said. He explained that it would be part of the symbolism. He moved forward and passed the bottle and cheese. I was startled when the bottle was passed to me. Although several of those who had handled it before me had placed it to their lips as if they were drinking, it was empty. The inside of the bottle was dry. We all ate the cheese. (Sellers, 138–39)

Ellington is not faced with this concern, but both men are in the process of discovering which traditions within the Afro-American panoply of political options can best define and direct their activism. For Moses and Ellington, certain fundamental questions about personality must be answered before their activism acquires consistency. Until then their activism is well-meaning eclecticism which confuses the individual and baffles onlookers.

Prospective members of the integrationist group that Sutherland and McDermott head are told that they are to read *One Hundred Years of Lynching* and to be prepared to discuss the book. White members are to read the book under the watchful eye of one of the black members. Sutherland questions one such member:

"Were you able to experience pain while reading the book?"

"Yes, I was . . ."

"How did it express itself?"

"I threw up."

"And did you continue reading?"

"Yes."

"Why?"

"I felt if black people could survive those horrible experiences, I could tolerate a bad taste in my mouth long enough to finish the book."

"Are you prepared to do anything else besides throwing up?"

"I know I can't undo what's already been done, but now that I've begun to experience black pain I am ready to be the instrument for whatever is required by the Movement."

"What about being white? How do you intend to deal with the resentment you'll face because you're white?"

"I am willing to do whatever is necessary to change that. And if I can't, I'll just have to accept it."

"I see." (Brown, 59)

The focus on individual commitment is part of the early thrust of civil rights organizations. Though white members of these organizations were vaguely aware of structural problems in the American political process, they felt that the force of individual will could change racist policies. One such white student, Jane Stembridge, who felt this way, has a point of view similar to the white woman Sutherland questions. Stembridge explains her involvement in SNCC: " 'Finally it all boils down to human relationships. It has nothing to do with governments. It is the question of whether we . . . whether I shall be a we.

The student movement is not a cause . . . it is a collision between this one person and that one person. It is am I going to sit beside you. . . . Love alone is radical. Political statements are not; programs are not; even going to jail is not' " (Zinn, 7). Although the acts of individual commitment on the part of the black and white student activists of the civil rights movement helped reshape this country, those acts exacted a tremendous toll on the individuals involved. Any act meant to change entrenched policies and actions of governments and people can be hard on the individuals involved, but in the case of the Jane Stembridges and Bob Moseses and fictional characters like Ellington, the toll is greater because they function on a historically illiterate plane. Their perspective creates narrow vision.

In talking about the formation of SNCC, Sellers, quoting Julian Bond, makes a similar point. Bond's comments concern the founding of SNCC and the reaction of soon-to-be SNCC members to Ella Baker's remarks at the founding meeting: " 'Although it was not well received, her speech was probably the best of the three' [Martin Luther King, Jr., and James Lawson were the other two speakers], said Julian Bond. Her thesis was 'More Than a Hamburger;' that what we were up to was more than just eating a hamburger at a lunch counter. She said that we ought to be interested in a whole range of social problems that dealt with black people; that lunch counter protests were the first step towards involving ourselves in this whole process" (Sellers, 36). The "whole process" and the "social problems" to which Baker refers are of course historical; the struggle to sit at lunch counters is part of an ongoing struggle for full democratic rights. The failure of the students initially to realize the larger dimensions of the movement resulted from the overemphasis on individual commitment to the exclusion of historical study.

After Sutherland completes his questioning of the white student, McDermott questions the black student, Melvin Ellington. McDermott asks Ellington if he wants to deal with history, and Ellington answers no. For Ellington, history is not relevant. But McDermott will make history clear to him by explaining why movement members do not wear neckties: " 'Wearing ties is a form of contemporary lynch laws. In other words, it's the rope revisited. They are part of the official uniform of oppression, lynching people to stifling jobs and choking their identity. Having this perspective forces us to commit a kind of suicide by murdering our capacity to cop out;" (Brown, 60). Ellington is impressed: "Theo [Sutherland] and Keith [McDermott] seemed to have thought it all out, complete with contingency theses for tightening up any snags in their arguments" (Brown, 61).

The integrationist politics of Sutherland and McDermott, particularly their characterization of themselves as the second line of defense for the civil rights workers in the South, is very similar to the stand of student civil rights organizations during the early sixties. Partially because the members of such organizations chose to personalize the struggle, they tended to romanticize activities necessary to achieve social change. Sellers discusses one faction within SNCC: "The most flamboyant faction was composed of a group of 'stars,' who at various time were referred to a 'philosophers, existentialists, anarchists, floaters and freedom-high niggers. . . .' They were high on Freedom, against all forms of organization and regimentation" (Sellers, 131). Sutherland's group adopts the name of this faction for one of its activities. He explains their "freedom highs," which are described as parties, to a prospective member: " 'Well, we call them "freedom highs" because everybody is supposed to slide their fantasies up under somebody else. If the other person digs it, then they both experience it until they get enough. And that's freedom high. It's just a way to get all the bullshit out of their system. If you analyze it, you'll see it's not as fucked up as it sounds. It's all political' " (Brown, 61). What these functions actually do is provide a political basis for interracial love affairs. During the early days of SNCC such activity was but another instance of racial progress. "Integration was their goal and the hero during the early stages of Snick was Bill Hansen, a white liberal who married a Negro girl and went to work for the organization in Arkansas to organize Negroes and to defy local marriage customs" (Roberts, 122). The fictional treatment of freedom high is similar to the way the term was used among some SNCC members.

Generally, however, freedom high in the novel and in the real world is characterized by lumpy mixtures of various unappropriated and thinly understood philosophies. Logical contradictions between Frantz Fanon's concept of righteous violence and Albert Camus's notions of rebellious absurdity did not stop early SNCC members from quoting freely from both (Roberts, 29). These people had no apparent need for theoretical consistency, only a desire to critique American society to illustrate its hypocrisy. Structural questions concerning the ability and willingness of a capitalist and racist country to extend democratic rights in all areas, including the economy, were not raised. Julian Bond writes concerning this phase: " 'It wasn't that there was no one to our left; there was. . . . We just were not ready. We were into our thing. To our mind, lunch counter segregation was the greatest evil facing black people in the country and if we could eliminate it, we would be like gods' " (Sellers, 45). Early SNCC members simply wanted America to live up to its promise of equality.

The absence of a unified theoretical framework not only made Fanon and Camus heroes of equal merit and instruction, but it opened the door for elevating individual fantasies to the level of serious politics:

> Last year, two Snick members—Scott B. Smith and Jesse Harris—began to wear necklaces of bones fastened with rawhide, and the word quickly circulated that perhaps some new philosophy had developed in Snick. Conversations with Harris, Smith and their friends weren't very enlightening, though, as they were likely one day to say that the bones represented the remains of Jefferson Davis, and the next day explain that they were part of a voodoo ritual, or brought good luck. Just as some whites were beginning to wonder if Harris and Smith didn't herald an American answer to the Mau Mau, both men took jobs in the Federal antipoverty program and are now looked upon by some Snick members as middle class. (Roberts, 122)

Smith and Harris do not represent the whole of SNCC, but when their actions are seen along with the group's other changes, it appears that philosophical eclecticism results from an individual's attempt to discover his/her personality within an activist context. This is not to suggest that these individuals did not have a sense of self before becoming activists but that their sense of self was sufficiently unsettled to result in projections of their actions that were at least confusing, if not contradictory.

Given the enormous, complicated, and still unfinished task of making America a democracy for all, it is understandable that SNCC members were not always able to speak with a single voice or that individuals sometimes explained the same phenomena in different ways. The theoretical and organizational consistency normally associated with groups that seek to restructure a society was not always apparent, but there were not then nor are there now clear organizational or theoretical models for restructuring American society. Thus it is a tribute to individual commitment and, ironically, to organizational tenacity that SNCC was able to have the impact that it had.

Just as organizations seek to discover models in the racial past of their members to enable them to maximize their potential, so must individual activists seek such models in their individual, family, and racial histories. Discovering oneself in a historical context is necessary to health. Clearly this is the lesson the fictional Ellington must learn, and it is not unlike the lesson Robert Moses and others like him had to learn. This is not a criticism but an acknowledgment that political activism works to peel back personality so that it is essential that self-understanding be anchored in the context of one's personal and racial history.

When Malcolm X is assassinated, Ellington is made to focus on the void that Sutherland's "contingency theses" are unable to fill. Sutherland's response—especially his reconsideration of his own personal history and his consequent turn to nationalism—is similar to that of many Afro-Americans to Malcolm's assassination. Because Malcolm X never had the opportunity to develop his new political program, his death was made to serve the often contradictory desires of the living. Everyone had the last word on the direction his life was taking at that time. In this sense, his death raised more questions than it answered, providing an opportunity for a range of activities to be carried out under the banner of his martyrdom. For Sutherland, Malcolm's death occasions a political soul-searching that nullifies the earlier usefulness of the integrationist movement. Sutherland speaks at a memorial service: " 'Too often we use coming together like this as a kind of moral lightning rod instead of a looking glass. None of us can afford to take refuge in the role of speaker or spectator. We must cease being mere fans of the activity of life and make engagement the substance out of which our lives are made' " (Brown, 67). The initial engagement is a disengagement from the politics of the integrationist movement and an advocacy of an unusual form of cultural nationalism. The Blue Monks attempt to emulate the changes and eccentricities of Theolonius Monk's music.

Intended or not, the esoteric nature of the Blue Monks' problack stance has interesting parallels with the new black power SNCC and with Ron Karenga's US. With SNCC, the open-ended theory formulation around the idea of black power allowed a range of eccentricities to be paraded as distinctively black (Long). Everything was possible, and the media absorbed and distorted each theory that was presented. Karenga's group was extreme in its symbolic use of per-ceived indigenous African cultural expressions such as names and clothing. The various ceremonies they created were a blending of tradition (derived from the African past) and reason (derived from the American experience) (Karenga, 15–22).

An important distinction between Karenga, the black power SNCC, and other such organizations is the systematic nature of US's theoretical formulations and the discipline displayed by its members. Both these factors may account for US's continued existence and the continued influence of its theoretical formulations on Afro-American cultural life. The most obvious indication of its influence is the attention various organizations and Afro-American politicians pay to the question of a "black value system" (usually some variant of the Nguzo Saba), a concept that was central to US's political activism. Additionally, the celebration of Kwanza, which is an Afro-American alternative to Christmas, remains high among Afro-Americans ("Cel-ebrate! Make Your Holidays Black and Beautiful"; "Merry Kwanza"). Individuals and organizations that assert the need for a black value system or celebrate Kwanza are unlikely to trace those activities back to US. In part, this is a result of the almost endemic difficulty Afro-Americans have in institutionalizing and projecting the products of their imaginations. Each generation of black women and men seems destined to reconstruct Afro-American history as opposed to building on traditions that are an ongoing part of their education.

The looseness that characterized the early black power or black pride movement resulted from an absence of black institutional development, a complicated issue that deserves fuller treatment than it will get here. The point I wish to make is that this looseness allowed many individuals to advance attitudes and actions that in-dicated more about the extent to which the American experience had deformed them than about any agreed-upon notion of what intrinsic blackness might be. This assertion will be more fully developed in the second part of the book; here it is sufficient to note that there is a connection between individual oddity, which parades as serious pol-itics, and an absence of a clear theoretical framework. The two exist symbiotically. Without a clear theoretical framework "everything becomes everything" in a sometimes maddening array of eclectic equality.

Sutherland's transformation means that he and McDermott can

no longer work together. McDermott acknowledges this and then goes on to tell Sutherland, " 'You can't shut me out of history, I'm still part of the struggle.' " Sutherland replies that he is not and then instructs McDermott to buy a book of matches, set himself on fire, and then shake hands with President Johnson. McDermott answers: " 'Your real problem, Theo, is that you've never been able to get over the fact that you pushed Geneva [Sutherland's black girlfriend] and me together before you changed the rules of freedom high. And now that you've made the game all black, it fucks you up that she didn't come back to you but decided to stay with me' " (Brown, 68–69). Sutherland's response is to beat McDermott senseless.

The internal sniping in SNCC when whites were expelled did not reach such pugilistic heights, but there was drama. In 1967 after all but one white had been ousted from any position of influence in SNCC, the organization's newspaper published a story critical of Zionism, noting that the struggle of the Palestinian people was similar to that of black people. The Jewish response was hostile: "Perhaps the unkindest cut . . . came from actor–folk singer Theodore Bikel, a member of SNCC who resigned last week. Bikel was reminded of Mickey Schwerner and Andrew Goodman, the two young New York Jews who were lynched in 1964. " 'You have no right to spit on their tombs. They died for a concept of brotherhood which you now cover with shame' " ("SNCC and the Jews"). Cleve Sellers writes concerning the reaction of SNCC members to Bikel's "resignation": "Aside from his faulty logic, the thing that most surprised us about Bikel's letter was his belief that he could resign from SNCC. If he had been a member of the organization for five years—as he claimed—none of us knew anything about it" (Sellers, 202). The press did much to dramatize the cases of dedicated white liberals, always a minority within SNCC, who were let go by SNCC or whose responsibilities were diminished. The changes black organizations and individuals underwent during the sixties were often a result of the struggle to find the right combination of racial precedent and personal attributes that could help them obtain freedom and literacy. The sometimes awesome changes that typified the actions of some SNCC members and fictional characters such as Sutherland are best understood in this light.

Still, within this vortex, Ellington has not reflected on what it all means. He has lightly questioned Sutherland, but he still follows him into the next phase, the "No Vietnamese Ever Called Me a Nigger Caucus." The purpose of this organization is to heighten the contradictions in American society by drafting members and then having them refuse induction. Sutherland assumes that the majority of Americans will be transformed when the state brings its repressive force down to crush their rebellion. This does not happen, and Sutherland's response is to go underground while Ellington, finally having grown tired of following other people's imperatives, marches off to prison.

In prison he mellows a bit but does not complete his growth. When he gets out of prison, a reunion with Otis and Otis's death provide the occasion for his maturation. Dr. Blue, who repairs the wound Ellington receives during the altercation in which Otis loses his life, asks Ellington why he went to prison instead of to Vietnam. Ellington's standard response, that he wanted to be the one to decide whether his life should be put on the line, does not satisfy Dr. Blue, who then engages Ellington in an exchange that suggests the absurdity of any specific action. Dr. Blue says: " 'My being here [in the emergency room at the hospital] doesn't change a thing. What I do could be good, bad, or indifferent. It still doesn't make any difference' " (Brown, 164).

Dr. Blue's views are presented metaphorically through jazz and therefore avoid a strict advocacy of absurdity. He tells Ellington that he plays a Miles Davis tune, "So What," for people he thinks it will benefit. The tune starts with the various instruments competing for the listener's attention. The resulting conflict "speaks of bad news." But instead of the conflict becoming an absolute antagonism in which competition is to be crushed, it settles into a smooth symbiosis. Each instrument accepts in a "signifying" fashion what the other has to say:

> The bass is put out by the way everybody ganged up on him but he takes it out on the keyboard, saying "Hey, man, I just thought I'd pull your coat, but since you wanna get the ass I'm gonna sic Miles on you. . . ." His solo is a wolf ticket signifying behind the dozens, with a little of my father talking mean through his teeth and biting down on his lower lip. The tenor man takes his solo out, murder-mouthin the "so what" piano chord. . . . But the piano man ain't impressed, saying in so many words, "Yeah, I hear you but ain't nobody put their hands on me." So the answer is still "So what."
> (Brown, 136)

The individual instruments' acceptance of their contributions to the music without becoming antagonistic becomes the metaphor for Ellington's life. He can now devise his own arrangements. His life becomes an approach, a style that is sufficiently fluid to adjust and respond to the unexpected. Primary to this style is a self-acceptance that releases Ellington's nascent jazz paradigm.

Ellington is similar to Ben in *Coming Home* in that it is doubtful that he will become a fervent revolutionary in the tradition of Abraham Blackman in *Captain Blackman*. But he has found space for himself outside the confusion that characterizes his activism. This space is within an important Afro-American tradition, music.

The use of metaphorical solutions for life's very real problems in a sense guided the civil rights movement. In its most general formulation, religion is a metaphorical system that answers questions and provides a code of behavior. The metaphor becomes real as people seek to live it. Thus a life modeled on the improvisations of Miles Davis can be a marvelous beginning for an individual too long under the sway of other people's magic.

The development of Ellington's character allows a glimpse into the integrationist, nationalist, and antiwar movements among blacks and whites during the sixties. The metaphorical resolution to the problem activism caused or exacerbated is instructive, and it foreshadows the actions of characters discussed in the second part of this book.

The preceding chapters have shown that black soldiers who were able to see themselves in a generalized historical context were less psychologically mangled than were those who viewed their situation in a purely individualized manner. Historical literacy enabled individuals to move beyond the boundaries that Vietnam, and all that term connotes, proscribed. Like so much of Afro-American life, Vietnam was a contradictory experience from which the black soldier could learn and grow or not learn and continue to assume that belonging to America was actually dependent on his actions.

References

Berry, Mary, and John W. Blassingame. *Long Memory: The Black Experience in America.* New York: Oxford University Press, 1982.

Brown, Wesley. *Tragic Magic.* New York: Random House, 1978.

"Celebrate! Make Your Holidays Black and Beautiful." *Essence,* December 1982, pp. 93–96.

Cowley, S. L., and M. Lord. "Merry Kwanza." *Newsweek,* 19 December 1977, p. 103.

Foner, Jack D. *Blacks and the Military in American History.* New York: Praeger, 1974.

Karenga, Maulana Ron. *Kawaida Theory: An Introductory Outline.* Inglewood, Calif.: Kawaida Publications, 1980.

Long, Richard. "The Symbolization of Black Consciousness: Anatomy of a Failure." CASS Occasional Paper 12. Atlanta: Center for African and African-American Studies, Atlanta University, n.d.

Nordheimer, Jon. "From Dakko to Detroit: Death of a Troubled Hero." In *The Black Soldier, from the American Revolution to Vietnam,* edited by Jay David and Elaine Crane. New York: Morrow, 1971. Pp. 228–46.

Roberts, Gene. "The Story of Snick: From 'Freedom High' to 'Black Power.' " *New York Times Magazine,* 25 September 1966, pp. 27–29, 119–20, 122, 124, 126, 128.

Sellers, Cleve. *River of No Return.* New York: Morrow, 1973.

"SNCC and the Jews." *Newsweek,* 24 August 1967, p. 22.

Taliaferro, B. S. "Celebrating Kwanza: One Family's Story." *Essence,* December 1983, p. 103.

White, F. "The New Soul Christmas." *Ebony,* December 1983, pp. 29–30.

Zinn, Howard. *SNCC: The New Abolitionists.* Boston: Beacon Press, 1964.

PART II

Novels of the Civil Rights
and Black Power Movements

5

The Civil Rights and Black Power Movements:
An Overview

The civil rights and black power movements illustrate the complex nature of the Afro-American struggle for self-definition during the sixties. Alice Walker's *Meridian* and John McCluskey's *Look What They Done to My Song,* two novels in which characterization and plot are shaped by the civil rights movement, explore the possibility that the black church might achieve the goals of that movement—particularly the goal of integration. John Killens's *The Cotillion or One Good Bull Is Half the Herd* and Ishmael Reed's *The Last Days of Louisiana Red,* two novels in which characterization and plot are shaped by the black power movement, explore the possibility that black spirituality might achieve the goals of the black power movement—particularly some aspect of self-definition based on nationalism.

The black church and black spirituality are related in that both seek fundamental answers to life's opportunities and problems, but they differ in approach. The black church here means a specific place of worship whose practices can be identified as essentially Christian, though the practice of that Christianity may have more in common with the Old Testament than the New in the tendency of its practitioners to appeal directly to God as opposed to using Jesus as an intermediary. Black spirituality shares the black church's tendency to appeal directly to God, but it differs in its reliance on beliefs outside

Christianity, particularly various forms of ancestor worship and what is usually referred to as voodoo.

Within the considerable historical boundaries of the black church and black spirituality, characters in all four novels seek some precedent that can help them clarify the consequences of their activism and can also help them advance the struggle for freedom and literacy.

The major characters in the civil rights novels are naive and sensitive individuals who are often left speechless by the pedestrian reality to which their peers so deftly respond. Getting and holding jobs, deciding what to do with one's life, choices about romantic relationships, all the decisions associated with maturity defy their understanding. Their world is without order or precedent. Then something happens—an assassinatioin or a brutal confrontation with the police—that changes these characters. A veil of ignorance is lifted, and they see the world clearly for the first time. They seek the company of their peers, and together with their peers they launch various forays into self- and historical understanding. They become activists whose achievements are various. The movement from lethargy and into activism is far more important to a character's development than is the relative success of that activism.

Even before a climactic and consiousness-changing event occurs, there is something special about the major characters in the two civil rights novels. Although they falter, it is clear that their destiny will take them beyond their initial ignorance and confusion and into some form of leadership. Meridian becomes a "griot." She recognizes the necessity of informing each generation of the struggles of previous generations so as to keep the story of the people alive. She realizes this need through attending the black church. Mack, the major character in McCluskey's novel, also relies on the black church to shape and determine the form his leadership will take. He becomes a minister in a synthetic church that fuses the traditional Afro-American religion with the requirements of the civil rights movement.

The characters in the civil rights novels who stand outside the influence of the black church never move beyond the boundaries that American society proscribes for black people. These characters operate in a field of immediacy that is similar to that in which the maladaptive black Vietnam veteran operated. The maladaptive civil rights character, however, has more options than his Vietnam counterpart and as a result can achieve a modicum of material success. These characters, however, become mired in pursuit of the American Dream—a profession, a home in the suburbs, or membership in an exclusive club. This pursuit results from their having modified the rhetoric of the civil rights movement in a way that allows them to seek traditional bourgeois occupations. But the life their activism opens makes it impossible for them fully to pursue their careers. In effect, they always return to the scene of their initiation into activism to discover what went wrong. Operating outside any aspect of the tradition of the black church makes these characters predictable and unhappy.

The black power characters are more sophisticated than the civil rights characters in that they never believe in America's dream of equality based on merit. They thus begin their activism with more historical literacy than do the civil rights characters. Their development is effected by reclaiming the magic associated with a people's historical perception of themselves. Historical literacy becomes a basis for racial positive thinking. The characters discussed in this second part of the book who were able to shape events and control history were those who went to the core of black religion. Affiliation with a traditional religious institution is not necessary. Rather, these characters adapt traditional African religion—some variant of voodoo—into a new organizational form. In Reed's novel, for example, the organization to which the characters who control their history belong is called Solid Gumbo Works (SGW). Although it is never clear exactly what SGW manufactures and sells, it is clear that it functions as a metaphorical solution to problems caused by an absent or improper historical perspective. Killens's novel focuses less on organizations than on the consequences of aligning oneself with a particular set of symbols. Predictably, those who are adept at using symbols associated with Afro-American life have the most African values or spirituality. But it is not the outward use of symbols—Afro hairstyles, African dress, and the like—but their meaning that determines the level of historical literacy among these characters. A version of African communalism in which the needs of the community override the desires of the individual best describes the meanings associated with the symbols in Killens's novel. Characters who adopt some aspect of African spirituality are able to exercise self-determination, which is the primary goal of the black power movement.

The maladaptive black power characters are fantastic chameleons who are able to rationalize whatever veneer expediency makes necessary. They are alternately rapists, leaders of radical organizations, celebrities, and artists. Obviously, these characters are not totally sincere about their activism. Mamadou Zero in Killens's novel and Street Yellings in Reed's novel are excellent examples. The minor characters in these novels are deformed by racism and are unable to articulate the cause and pain of that deformity. These characters have personality problems that precede their activism, and their involvement in the black power movement is an attempt to exorcise their deformity. The destruction and sadness that the major and minor characters in this group cause among their fictive peers is engulfing.

The plots of the civil rights novels are much more literal than are those in the black power novels because the goals of the civil rights movement—particularly integration—were part of the accepted version of the American Dream. The characters are simply asking America to live up to her promise. Therefore, the plots rely on a series of disappointments that point out the contradiction of America's promise of equality and the reality of racism. In illustrating this contradiction, the authors are more concerned with verisimilitude than are those who write the black power novels.

The plots of the black power novels are more fantastic than those of the civil rights novels because the authors go beyond the possibilities implicit in the American Dream. Killens and Reed believe that integration is possible only within an African or Afro-American framework. To get beyond the possibilities of the American Dream requires formulating plots that do not rely on the prejudices and opportunities of that dream; rather, the plots in their novels rely on various aspects of African and Afro-American history to give them structure. These plots are pre- or extralogical and do not depend on any contradiction between America's promise of equality based on merit and its reality of racism.

The focus of the black power novels is more didactic than is that of the civil rights novels in that the plots of the former are allegorical. Consequently, history is either presented as it is in *Captain Blackman,* which combines actual characters from history and historical events with fictive accounts, or it is presented in a conspiratorial fashion. The result in both instances is to make the reader question received versions of history. Reed does this more dramatically than does Killens.

If we consider all of Reed's fiction, some of the perplexing problems that have faced humankind could be posed as questions: Can struggles between different societies be understood as struggles between seceret societies with conflicting ideologies, each hoping to gain ascendancy? Are the problems that blacks face a result of evil spirits evoked by mean-spirited whites and ignorant blacks?

Killens develops his novel within the framework of the contradiction between appearance and reality by raising questions abut the meaning of symbols. He suggests that his readers consider blackness as an essence which has multitudinous expressions that cannot be encased in static symbols. In his novel, essence is a process defined by love for black people.

The education of the civil rights characters is fairly straightforward and can best be understood by thinking of these individuals responding to and ultimately shaping events. The characters who shape history are those who are positively associated with the black church. The education of the black power characters is more subtle and esoteric. They are required to recover secrets of the race's past and to apply them in a way that allows black people to control their lives. So, in a sense, we are not so much watching the development of a character as that of a race. The four novels that are examined in the following chapters help us to understand how civil rights and black power activists made sense of their lives after their particular movement had lost its momentum and also illustrate ways that fictive characters advanced the quest for freedom and literacy.

The major characters in the civil rights novels go through a process of development useful to understanding the ideological changes among black college students who were involved in the Student Non-Violent Coordinating Committee and other organizations with similar goals. The process the fictive characters undergo has four distinct stages: (1) they begin in darkness, a preliterate stage in which historical reflection—the attempt to understand oneself in the context of history—is absent or, in the better moments, is the most casual of occurrences; (2) their world shifts as a result of some catastrophic events; (3) they then become activists, determined to make America live up to its promise of equality based on merit; (4)

they finally enter the stage of reflection, atttempting to understand the successes and failures of their activism in a historical context.

The examples of the characters in the novels are extreme and are rarely precisely duplicated by men and women who participated in the civil rights movement. Nevertheless, these stages of development are useful to understanding the ideological shifts that occurred in the part of the civil rights movement dominated by students.

The naiveté and ignorance that characterize the first stage of development in the fictional characters is apparent in the early activities of black students who participated in the civil rights movement. The class standing of black student activists was the primary cause for their ignorance regarding the problems involved in effecting social change. In the first place, their status as college students placed them in a select group among their peers within the Afro-American community. Many of these students were the sons and daughters of successful black men and women and consequently did not know struggle the way most black men and women their ages did. Indeed, they were being prepared to carry on in the family tradition. Some of the parents of these activist students demanded that their children not be involved in the civil rights movement. As Cleve Sellers notes, "Everyone had parent problems. . . . Although some objected more than others, none of our parents were happy with our decision to go to Mississippi. Upon hearing the news, most parents hit the ceiling" (Sellers, 78–79).

Although many of these students disregarded their parents' warnings about going to Mississippi to work for the Voter Education Project, thereby jettisoning some of their class preogatives, they still retained middle-class values. They still believed in the American system, as a 1960 SNCC leaflet demonstrates:

> We affirm the philosophical or religious ideal of nonviolence as the foundation of our purpose, the presupposition of our faith, and the manner of our action. Nonviolence as it grows from Judaeo-Christian traditions seeks a social order of justice permeated by love. Integration of human endeavor represents the crucial first step towards such a society.
>
> Through nonviolence, courage replaces fear, love transforms hate. Acceptance dissipates prejudice; hope ends despair. Peace dominates war; faith reconciles doubt. (Meier, Rudwick, and Broderick; 307)

Six years after making this statement, SNCC was calling for black power. Initially, however, SNCC members thought that social change could be accomplished by highlighting the contradiction between what America promised and what it actually delivered.

SNCC's assumptions in this regard also influenced its tactics, but in an inverse fashion. In organizing sit-ins, SNCC members assumed that their appearance as neat, well-mannered Negroes would give lie to the perception of blacks as slovenly and ill-mannered: "We were very concerned about the image. We wanted to show white people that we knew how to act and were, therefore, worthy of being where they ate. We were so conscious of image, in fact, that we probably would have turned down anyone who attempted to join the demonstration while attired in a sweat shirt" (Sellers, 22). Many of the early leaders of the student civil rights movement wanted to convince whites that they were just like whites. Although the concern with appearance has an obvious tactical dimension by removing one line of defense that whites may have used in denying blacks public access to various businesses and services, it also indicates that these students saw themselves through white eyes. It never occurred to them that they might actually be superior to the group with which they were trying to integrate. The students thought they had to prove themselves worthy to the white world, but they never looked critically at that world; they never questioned its worth.

The integrationist, almost assimilationist, values of the early civil rights activists, those operating from 1960 until 1963, were in tune with the national rhetoric concerning the civil rights movement. If articles in news and popular magazines are used as a measure, during this period the national rhetoric was openly advocating the right of blacks to participate fully in the most basic of democratic rights, the right to vote. Some representative titles are as follows: "Right to Vote a Must" (1960), "What Congress Plans to Do about Negro Rights" (1960), "Within the Framework" (1960), "Liberty in Peril" (1961), "Fights Not Over" (1961), "For Negro Rights" (1961), "Push for Civil Rights" (1963), "Inevitable Process" (1963). The articles under these titles spoke approvingly of full democratic rights for blacks.

The integrationist thrust of the civil rights activists attracted a coterie of beautiful and famous people who had previously distinguished themselves in all fields of endeavor save that of race relations. All of a sudden everyone had an opinion on civil rights. A white student who joined SNCC explained his rationale: " 'I have never felt so intense, alive, such a sense of well-being, which is not to be confused with the illusion of "happiness" equated to "having fun." I have chosen to be outside of society after having been very much inside. I intend to fight that society which lied to and smothered me for so long, and continues to do so to vast number of people. . . . My plans are unstructured in regards to anything but the immediate future. I believe in freedom and must take the jump; I must take the chance of action' " (Zinn, 15). Though obviously more intense and exuberant than most, this student's desire to extend democratic rights to Afro-Americans is representative of the feelings of many Americans.

The unabashed enthusiasm of this student and others, black and white, was eventually altered by the brutality of southern whites who were determined not to allow blacks to exercise their constitutional rights. Cleve Sellers discusses the changes that SNCC underwent from its inception until 1966:

> During the first phase, which lasted from 1960 through 1962, SNCC's members were largely middle class and very religious. They were primarily interested in securing integrated public accommodations and basic dignity for blacks. Depending on courtesy and a Ghandian ability to take punishment, they were basically successful.
>
> SNCC entered its second phase when it sent organizers to Mississippi to register rural blacks. Many of those who joined the organization during this period, which roughly lasted from 1962 through the Democratic National Convention in August, 1964, saw themselves as guerilla organizers. I was one of them. . . . SNCC entered a third stage after Atlantic City. That stage lasted until the spring of 1966, when Stokely Carmichael was elected chairman. (Sellers, 146–47)

Sellers's divisions are very useful in understanding the ideological shifts of this phase of the civil rights movement. From 1960 until approximaately 1963, the country was greatly enamored of the movement. The titles of articles mentioned above are one measure of that enthusiasm, and the fervor of many white students who went south to participate in sit-ins is another indicator.

Southern whites reacted violently to the attempt of black students to register southern blacks, and their attitude ultimately helped to push the movement in a nationalist direction with the call for black power replacing the call for integration. The response of the country, especially the government, to this brutality was not consonant with the egalitarian rhetoric. Writing in 1984 about the violence directed at Afro-Americans who tried to vote in Mississippi and at blacks and whites who encouraged them to register and vote, Paul Cowan notes:

> By 1964, the litany of black martyrs was already a long one. In Liberty, Mississippi, Herbert Lee and Lewis Allen had been slain for seeking to register; in Jackson, NAACP field secretary Medgar Evers had been assassinated because he was an effective leader of a voter education campaign. . . . But such acts went virtually unnoticed outside the black community, the small community of Northern integrationists, and some college campuses. There was a cruel indifference underlying the apathy. In 1962 and 1963, for instance, after Herbert Lee and Lewis Allen were murdered, the brilliantly persuasive SNCC leader Bob Moses couldn't convince Attorney General Robert Kennedy to order FBI agents to come to Liberty, Mississippi, and protect blacks who sought the franchise. (Cowan, 11)

Even as the media extolled the need to extend basic democratic rights to blacks, it ignored the price that blacks were paying to exercise those rights. Cowan goes on to say that David Dennis, a SNCC leader, reasoned that the country would continue to ignore black deaths and that the only way to focus attention on black enfranchisement was for white students, especially white women, to be involved and to risk their lives. Dennis says: " 'The idea was to . . . get the country to begin to respond to what was going on down there. They were not going to respond to a thousand blacks working that area. They would respond to a thousand white college students, and white college females who were down there. . . . [If] it took some deaths to do it, the death of a white college student would bring more attention to what was going on' " (Cowan, 11). Though cold, Dennis's observations were accurate. In 1964, Andrew Goodman and Mickey Schwerner and a black man, James Chaney, were murdered in Mississippi. "Those murders—and the publicity the Freedom Summer generated—created the climate of opinion Dave Dennis and Bob Moses had foreseen. The outrage intensified by the beatings and murders that occurred in Selma, Alabama, the next March. It helped prompt President Johnson to introduce the 1965 voting rights bill" (Cowan, 11). During this period, SNCC underwent an inevitable radicalization process. Its members learned, among other things, that black life was still secondary to white life. Public opinion concerning the need for blacks to exercise full democratic rights was not influenced by blacks sacrificing their lives for those rights. White lives were a higher sacrifice.

This lesson resulted in the further erosion of the American Dream, and the pivotal event was the treatment of the Mississippi Freedom and Democratic Party (MFDP) at the 1964 Democratic National Convention. SNCC organized Mississippi precinct by precinct to put together a delegation in hopes of unseating the regular white-controlled delegation that Mississippi sent to the convention. Members of SNCC had carefully documented the systematic oppression of blacks in Mississippi, the changes they had to make to be able to vote, their living conditions; in short, they documented the sociopolitical culture of Mississippi to show that blacks had been systematically locked out of the process of delegate selection. They intended to take their challenge to the Democratic party at the convention. The party listened and offered a compromise; the MFDP would be given two nonvoting seats within the regular Mississippi delegation. The MFDP refused.

SNCC followed all the rules in documenting its case; its member tried to be good Americans, and they were patronized in the most ironic of ways. The compromise offered by the Democratic party simply ignored the right of blacks to vote. Racism meant that no black organization could participate equally in the "democratic" process. Cleve Sellers writes about SNCC members' feelings after the convention: "The national Democratic party's rejection of the MFDP at the 1964 convention was to the civil rights movement what the Civil War was to American history: afterward things could never be the same. Never again were we lulled into believing the task was exposing injustices so that the 'good' people of America could eliminate them. We left Atlantic City with the knowledge that the movement had turned into something else. After Atlantic City, our struggle was not for civil rights, but for liberation" (Sellers, 111). The changes that Sellers foresaw did not immediately make their way into the national consciousness. Part of the reason was the success of the march on Washington and the passing of the voting rights bill.

During this period, however, SNCC was becoming increasingly nationalistic, and it was beginning to focus attention on international issues. It was among the first organizations to speak against black participation in the Vietnam War. By this time, 1966, the civil rights movement was in some disarray, for its goals and tactics were being routinely questioned by many blacks. There were very clear competing centers of power. Again, the headlines in news and popular magazines reflected the absence of consensus. The following titles are representative: "Line in the Dust: Movement Split Down the Middle" (1966), "Negro Leaders Dividing: The Effect" (1966), "Pharaoh's Lessons: Fighting among Themselves" (1966), "Crisis in Civil Rights Leadership" (1966), "Here Lies Integration" (1966).

The shift in public opinion reflected in these titles resulted from the nationalist thrust of SNCC and other such organizations. The move toward nationalism was a clear move away from the American Dream with its implicit assumption of advancement based on merit. A 1967 SNCC leaflet stands in stark contrast to the 1960 leaflet quoted earlier: "The black man in America is in a perpetual state of slavery no matter what the white man's propaganda tells us. . . . We are not alone in this fight, we are a part of the struggle for self-definition of all black men everywhere. We here in America must unite ourselves to be ready to help our brothers elsewhere. We must fight to gain BLACK POWER here in America" (Meier, Rudwick; and Broderick; 484–85). SNCC changed from an integrationist to a nationalist organization.

Summarizing the meanings of the civil rights movement, Ron Karenga writes:

> A critical analysis of the civil rights struggle, reveal[s] a series of major accomplishments . . . its first and perhaps most important achievement was increased liberalization of the U.S. system. Through legal, economic and political challenges, Blacks were able to achieve among other things: 1) the 1954 Brown decision; 2) the Civil Rights Act of 1957; 3) the 1960 Civil Rights Bill; 4) the Interstate Commerce Commission ruling in September, 1961, against segregation on interstate carriers and terminals; 5) the Civil Rights Act of 1964 which was the most far-reaching and comprehensive civil rights bill passed by Congress; 6) mass voter registration; 7) the 1965 Voting Rights Act; and 8) widespread desegregation of public facilities. (Karenga, *Introduction to Black Studies*, 131–32)

Although some of the accomplishments that Karenga notes preceded SNCC, they all resulted from the same movement. The personal risks involved in accomplishing these goals and the changes undergone by college-age Afro-Americans in the process are the focus of the two novels in which characterization and plot are shaped by the civil rights movement. The actions of characters in these novels provide insight to understanding the actions of individuals in the real world who were involved in the civil rights movement.

The novels that provide the basis for discussing the black power movement deal with two aspects of that movement: the necessity to separate appearances from reality and intraracial conflict resulting from an absence of theoretical clarity about problem conceptualization and resolution on the part of individuals or organizations involved.

The first aspect, the distinction between appearance and reality, is developed in Killens's novel. Killens uses the cotillion as a central symbol to explore a range of other symbols that are associated with being black in the sixties. He illustrates the tenuousness of assigning a high degree of political consciousness to black women and men who wore natural hairstyles or African attire. The characters in Killens's novel must learn that artifacts are not windows to the soul and consequently are not indicative of how black women and men might treat each other.

The second aspect of the black power movement, the theme of intraracial conflict, is treated most fully in Reed's novel. Such conflicts can lead to racial betrayal; they can foster revolutionary nihilism; or they can deepen problems between black women and men. In each instance, the character or group of characters involved lacks theoretical clarity, so their actions can take bizarre and often self-defeating turns. Nationalism and Marxism, the two major ideologies of the period, are satirized in Reed's novel because of the way they were practiced during the sixties; in particular, their static conceptions of reality impeded advancement of the quest for freedom and literacy and undervalued individual personality in a march toward increasing levels of uniformity.

Within the context of these two aspects of the black power movement, the major characters undergo a three-part evolution. Even though they begin with a higher degree of historical literacy than do the characters in the civil rights novels, they are still somewhat naive. Specifically, their confidence in the correctness of their philosophical assumptions and in their tactical approach to social change is shaken when their actions do not have the desired result. They are then forced to reflect, just as the characters in the civil rights novels do, to find a deeper approach to social change. They learn that the world requires more than one equation for understanding. After their reflection, they suggest new approaches to social changes and racial advancement. The new approaches are actually variations or updates of ancient lessons. The challenge that confronts these characters involves recasting ancient magic in modern forms. The plots and characterization of these novels suggest new ways of interpreting the black power movement.

The black power movement, which lasted approximately from 1966 until 1972, touched much of black and white America. Unlike the civil rights movement, however, it never enjoyed any positive press. From the beginning, the press reviled the movement with such headlines as "Major Turning Point against Negro Movement" (1966), "New Racism; Emphasis on Black Power" (1966), "Grasping at Chaos" (1967), and "Racial Crisis: A Consensus" (1967). Despite the negative reaction by the white press and by white America generally, this struggle for self-definition and self-determination did attract many black people. "Perhaps for the first time in black history, an enthusiastic and profoundly popular nationalist praxis had captured the overwhelming majority of the students, the unemployed, workers, and the elite. The nationalist worldview translated into popular music (e.g., James Brown's "I'm Black and I'm Proud"), art and literature; sports (e.g., the defiant Black Power statements of black athletes at the 1968 Olympic Games); personal clothing, hair styles (the Afro) and even greetings (the elaborate soul handshake and raised fist)" (Marable, 100). The black power movement was pervasive.

Stokely Carmichael, one of the architects of the black power movement, and Charles Hamilton, a black political scientist, defined black power as follows: "[Black power] is a call for Black people in this country to unite, to recognize their heritage, to build a sense of community. It is a call for black people to begin to define their goals, to lead their own organizations and to support those organizations. It is a call to reject the racist institutions and values of this society. The concept . . . rests on a fundamental premise. *Before a group can enter the open society, it must first close ranks.* By this, we mean that group solidarity is necessary before a group can operate effectively from a bargaining position of strength in a pluralistic society" (Carmichael and Hamilton, 44). Despite this statement, there was no agreed-upon definition of black power among various nationalist organizations. One consequence was that nationalist organizations with decidedly different emphases concerning the best way of understanding and changing America claimed to be operating in the name of black power. Revolutionary and cultural nationalists both claimed to be exercising black power, but they viewed the nature of American society in fundamentally different ways. The revolutionary nationalists, especially as illustrated by the Black Panther party under the leadership of Eldridge Cleaver, viewed America as being composed of competing classes. Racism, they felt, obscured this fact, and its elimination would unify the working class to overthrow the capitalist class. The cultural nationalists, however, especially as represented by US, saw America as a pluralist society composed of competing ethnic groups. From their perspective, social advancement for blacks could occur only after they solidified around a clear set of values. There were innumerable hybrids of revolutionary and cultural nationalist thought, and black power was the ideological blanket under which all the theories resided.

The eclecticism of the early stages of this movement is similar to that of the early stages of SNCC. An obvious reason is that some of the individuals who participated in SNCC also participated in the black power movement. Beyond that, however, a deeper reason was that many of the participants in the movement lacked literacy. Consequently, they were compelled to commit versions of mistakes that had already been made: " 'Black is beautiful' we shouted as if it had some magic meaning and could in an instant overthrow ignorance and undo centuries of mental and physical damage and defend us against the diabolical forces that gathered to protect themselves from the televised image of rantin' and recently aware nationalists and episodic revolutionaries. . . . Instead of objectively increasing the range and roots of Black Power, we held up our fists for the six o'clock news and shouted 'right on' or 'habiri gani' and went right on making the same mistakes" (Karenga, "Overturning Ourselves," 8). Karenga's comments provided an excellent outline for a discussion of the symbolization of black culture, and the resulting problem of distinguishing appearance from reality.

Just as the civil rights movement became fashionable among people whose commitment was limited to mere appearance, the black power movement attracted Afro-Americans who cared less about the issues raised by the idea of black power than about appearing current. Blackness was something that could be put on and taken off like clothes. Going to the Black Student Union meeting required a dashiki, a natural, and a medallion of "African" origin dangling from one's neck. And so it went: the black woman with a perm was not truly black; the black man without a dashiki was at best questionable. There were interminable arguments about who was the "blackest." The opportunist quickly knew the score and used that knowledge to his or her benefit, often appearing as the "black" representative wherever white money resided. The point I wish to make here is that the symbols were not tied to an agreed-upon system of behavior, and so those symbols could be applied to whatever motivation the person with the strongest rationale might wish to tie them to.

As is true with any movement, all action is not simply good or bad. The defiant assertion that "Black Is Beautiful" was a necessary step to prepare black men and women psychologically to assume greater control over the world. It was a stage preparatory to projecting a new world-view. But when these symbolic assertions are not given an institutional form (which is Karenga's point in the above quote), they stand ready for abuse. It is particularly difficult for a race to project a positive image of itself in America because of the one-dimensional quality of this society, but this projection is all but impossible when the race in question does not institutionalize its view of itself. A clear loss of control results; symbols and icons are made to serve faddish and often crude purposes.

Another example of the absence of control that blacks generally exercised over their symbols is apparent in the way they were co-opted by whites. The soul handshake, for example, was initially an intra-group form of greeting, intended to show brotherhood. I recall my surprise when in 1969 I first met a white college roommate whose hand I shook. He was appalled. I had not given him the authentic soul handshake; he immediately went to work teaching me how to shake hands properly. This personal anecdote was no doubt duplicated countless times during this period. More dramatically than at any other period in modern history, with the possible exception of the 1920s, the co-optation of black symbols during the sixties demonstrates the tenuous nature of associating consciousness with the manipulation of symbols.

The struggle for self-determination that fueled the black power movement affected the relationships among black women and men. Although the attempt to redefine relationships is a necessary part of any people's struggle for self-determination, the absence of clear ideological positions among the nationalist organizations meant that individuals and organizations advanced a variety of models and tagged them as authentically African. The religious nationalist organizations had clearly defined roles for women, generally subordinate to men. The revolutionary nationalists often exploited black women, sometimes even expecting them to satisfy the men's sexual desires upon demand. In the Black Panther party, these women were called "Sister Love." Ron Karenga, the dominant theorist of the cultural nationalist movement, wrote, "Male supremacy is based on three things; tradition, acceptance, and reason" (Karenga, *Quotable Karenga,* 28).

The issue of male supremacy usually arose on the question of who should lead the movement and who should lead the family. The Elijah Muhammed–led Black Muslims, Karenga's US, and Baraka's Congress of African People all placed women in subordinate positions that were more or less genetically prescribed (Giddings, 314–24). The Moynihan Report, written by President Richard Nixon's adviser Patrick Moynihan, served to inflame discussions about the roles of black women and men in that it argued that black women needed to step back and allow black men to take the lead. One of the victims of racism was being blamed for the results of racism. The atmosphere in 1965, when the report was issued, was highly charged, and one result was that many black women outside the nationalist movement seem to have adjusted their beliefs to deal with the controversy. For example, in 1969 Dorothy Height, head of the National Council of Negro Women, said, " 'The major concern of the Negro woman is the status of the Negro man and his need for feeling himself an important person' " (Giddings, 329). Height's position was not rare, for it reflected an attempt by one part of the Afro-American community to deal with the issue of male and female relations in an era of political change.

Any time a race of people is involved in the process of self-definition, the situation is volatile and open to exploitation by individuals who have questionable motives.

> I had known Baba Oserjeman through a host of image changes. He was Francis King from Detroit, a friend of Steve Korrets, when I first met him. He was always spoken of then, by his friends, as a kind of con man–hustler.

He wore English riding outfits and jophurs and affected a bit of an English accent. He than became Francisco Ray, Spanish for a minute. Then he became Serj Khingh, a little Indian, and he opened one of the first coffehouses on the Lower East Side, called Bhowani's Table, where some of us used to go. The next I heard of Oserjeman, he had become Nana Oserjeman of the Damballah Qwedo, "practicing the religion of our fathers." And finally (?) Baba Oserjeman, chief priest of the Yoruba Temple. (Baraka, 215–16)

Because of the perception among Afro-Americans that the Yoruba religion condones polygamy, this last incarnation became a basis for the sexual exploitation of black women by some black men.

Intraracial battles between black organizations created another problem during this period, and some of those battles featured actual shoot-outs. These battles were made worse and in some instances caused by the COINTELPRO surveillance program operated by the Federal Bureau of Investigation (Blackstock). The battles between the US organization and the Black Panther party are easily the most dramatic (Rogers), but there were other less dramatic affairs. Amiri Baraka writes about his visits to New York after having left the Haryou-funded black arts movement: "For a couple of months, whenever I came to New York I carried a sawed-off shotgun in my hunting jacket in such a way that I could put my hand on it, open the coat, and fire almost simultaneously. But happily I had no confrontations" (Baraka, 228–29). Baraka details the particulars that led to his decision to carry a shotgun, but what stands out, even by his own admission, is the craziness of the events that made carrying a weapon necessary. What is clearest about the Baraka episode and others like it is the random quality of the nihilism that animated some participants in the black power movement.

This nihilism resulted from an absence of theoretical clarity. In many instances, organizations defined their actions as they went along. This is not to say that no attention was paid to the question of theory but that changes in applied theory—ideology—did not always seem tied to reasoned study. Both phenomena seemed to result from conversions that were outside of logic.

The novels I discuss in which plot and characterization are shaped by the black power movement develop these issues in ways that demonstrate the centrality of historical understanding to dealing with problems caused by activism. Black spirituality is the part of Afro-American history that holds answers for fictional as well as real black power activists.

References

Baraka, Amiri. *The Autobiography of Leroi Jones.* New York: Freundlich Books, 1984.

Blackstock, Nelson. *COINTELPRO: The FBI's Secret War on Political Freedom.* New York: Vintage Books, 1975.

Carmichael, Stokely, and Charles V. Hamilton. *Black Power.* New York: Vintage Books, 1967.

Cowan, Paul. "Mississippi Freedom Summer 20 Years Later." *Village Voice,* 19 June 1984, pp. 1, 11–19, 36.

Cruse, Harold. *The Crisis of the Negro Intellectual.* New York: Morrow, 1967.

"Fights Not Over." *Commonweal,* 5 May 1961, p. 141.

"For Negro Rights." *America,* 13 May 1961, pp. 266–67.

Giddings, Paula. *When and Where I Enter: The Impact of Black Women on Race and Sex in America.* New York: Morrow, 1984.

"Grasping at Chaos." *Nation,* 27 November 1967, pp. 547–48.

"Inevitable Process." *Time,* 14 June 1963, pp. 23–24.

"Here Lies Integration." *National Review,* 27 December 1966, pp. 1305–6.

Karenga, Maulana. *Introduction to Black Studies.* Inglewood, Calif.: US Organization, 1982.

———. "Overturning Ourselves: From Mystification to Meaningful Struggle." *Black Scholar,* October 1972, pp. 6–14.

———. *The Quotable Karenga.* Los Angeles: US Organization, 1967.

Killens, John. *The Cotillion, or One Good Bull Is Half the Herd.* New York: Trident Press, 1971.

"Liberty in Peril." *Time,* 15 September 1961, pp. 24–25.

"Line in the Dust: Movement Split Down the Middle." *Newsweek,* 18 July 1966, pp. 23–24.

McCluskey, John. *Look What They Done to My Song.* New York: Random House, 1974.

Marable, Manning. *Blackwater: Historical Studies in Race, Class Consciousness, and Revolution.* Dayton, Ohio: Black Praxis Press, 1981.

"Major Turning Point against the Negro Movement." *U.S. News and World Report,* 15 August 1966, p. 46.

Meier, August, Elliot Rudwick, and Francis L. Broderick. *Black Protest Thought in the Twentieth Century.* 2d ed. New York: Bobbs-Merrill, 1965.

"Negroe Leaders Dividing: The Effect." *U.S. News and World Report,* 18 July 1966, pp. 31-34.

"New Racism; Emphasis on Black Power." *Time,* 1 July 1966, pp. 11–13.

"Push for Civil Rights." *U.S. News and World Report.* 7 October 1963, pp. 110–12.

"Pharaoh's Lessons: Fighting among Themselves." *Time,* 9 September 1966, p. 22.

"Racial Crisis: A Consensus." *Newsweek,* 21 August 1967, pp. 16–17.

Reed, Ishmael. *The Last Days of Louisiana Red.* New York: Random House, 1974.

"Right to Vote a Must." *Time,* 29 February 1960, p. 20.

Rogers, R. "Guns on Campus." *Nation,* 5 May 1969, pp. 558–60.

Rowan, Carl T. "Crisis in Civil Rights Leadership." *Ebony,* November 1966, pp. 27–30.

Sellers, Cleve. *River of No Return.* New York: Morrow, 1973.

Walker, Alice. *Meridian.* New York: Harcourt Brace Jovanovitch, 1976.

"What Congress Plans to Do about Negro Rights." *U.S. News and World Report,* 14 March 1960, pp. 46–48.

"Within the Framework." *Time,* 8 February 1960, p. 29.

Zinn, Howard. *SNCC: The New Abolitionists.* Boston: Beacon Press, 1964.

6

Meridian:
Answers in the Black Church

A lice Walker's *Meridian* brilliantly illustrates three aspects of Afro-American life as focused on and developed by the civil rights movement. Those three aspects are themes in the novel and can be defined as (1) a form of parental and institutional socialization that does not connect the individual to his or her history, (2) problems within relationships between black men and women, and (3) the ascendancy of the black power movement (nationalism) and the diminution of the civil rights movement (integration).

Through Meridian, the major character, we see the effects of a form of parental socialization that does not help the child connect herself with Afro-American history. The reason for the absence of parental socialization is that Meridian's parents have failed to realize their individual dreams, and this failure begins a pattern that is continued by institutionalized education. Both institutions, the family and the school system, work to fragment Meridian's personality, making it difficult for her to see herself as functioning within a historical context.

A second civil rights concern the novel develops involves problems and opportunities within relationships between black women and men. This part of the novel provides insight into understanding how relationships that were formed during this period worked or failed to work. An ancillary theme has to do with the pressure white women exert on relationships between black men and women. This part of the novel illustrates how the black man is largely culpable in the failure of such relationships because he is not clear about his romantic and political motivations in regard to the black woman. His motivations are confused, and so he is capable of hurting black women without ever knowing that he is doing so.

The third concern has to do with the way various characters deal with the move from the civil rights movement to the black power movement. This struggle fuses the other two concerns. The intensification of nationalist activity that occurred during the black power movement dramatically illustrated the consequences of various forms of socialization to which some black parents subjected their children, and it illustrated the consequences of institutionalized education. The consequences in both cases were negative: many black parents and practically all educational systems worked to separate blacks from their history rather than connecting them to that history. The forms of socialization worked to personalize the Afro-American experience, thereby removing the individual from the historical reservoir of lessons and options available within the culture.

The move from civil rights to black power demonstrated the priority of black self-determination in a pluralist society. The issue of relationships was also radicalized by the black power movement, resulting in a rhetoric that elevated black women to an idealized position which replaced white women as models to emulate. To be sure, black men did not always relate to black women on the basis of this idealization; but it was certainly a part of the accepted rhetoric of the era.

The way characters deal with this final concern demonstrates the levels of freedom and literacy they obtain. In both instances, the way characters relate to the black church is pivotal. Those characters who use the black church as a basis to locate some clarifying precedent that does not distort their personality advance the quest for freedom and literacy. The characters who do not use the lessons of the black church in their effort to deal with changes do not come close to actualizing their potential. They cannot obtain peace because they are alternately attracted to and repelled by their previous lives as activists.

The first theme developed in the novel *Meridian*—the alienating effects of parental and educational socialization—is a theme of darkness and illiteracy. The second theme—the problems in the ways black men and women relate to each other—is developed in the context of this darkness and illiteracy, causing innumerable problems. The move from the civil rights movement to the black power movement is the final theme, and it serves to intensify and clarify the problems of the first two themes. Those characters who are positively associated with the black church are able to advance the quest for freedom and literacy, whereas those lacking that association cannot.

Although these themes are developed through Meridian's character, Walker writes the novel from several points of view, which allows her to illustrate the general and specific aspects of the civil rights movement, from Meridian's innermost thoughts and feelings to a relatively stark portrayal of civil rights demonstrations. The novel's scope is reflected in its three-part organization—"Meridian," "Truman Held," and "Endings"—which moves geographically while shifting emotional focus from one constellation of events to another. The "Meridian" section is set in Georgia and takes us through the main character's adolescence, college years, and destructive relationships with Truman. "Truman Held" is set primarily in Mississippi and develops the relationship between Truman and his Jewish wife, Lynne, while exploring ways white women perceive of their relationships with black men in particular and black people in general. "Endings" is set in both the North and South and depicts Meridian's and Truman's attempts to adjust their personal histories to issues left unresolved by the civil rights movement.

The chapter titles reflect the events of the movement and their effects on those involved. Titles such as "Battle Fatigue," "Awakening," and "Free at Last" indicate feelings at various times within the movement. The themes of the chapters also provide a basis for viewing the actions of characters in both an allegorical and an individual manner. Meridian's mother, Mrs. Hill's ignorant attachment to symbols results from a past that limited her vision and development. She is an allegorical product of her past who serves the function of teaching lessons.

The length of chapters and the use of flashbacks within them demonstrate the disjointed nature of political change and help us to see the confusion and urgency that characters experience as they attempt to change the American social fabric. Events and their meanings do not parade by in a straight line to reveal the consequences of characters' actions. Walker's choice to write in a nonlinear and nonsequential fashion reflects the haphazard and unpredictable nature of the lives of many activists who were involved in the civil rights movement.

Meridian Hill has a loveless childhood dominated by a mother who marches to rhythms she never fully understands or appropriates, a father whose sensitivity is never translated into any instructive bond, and an immature husband whose desires oscillate between the necessity of having creased jeans and frequent sexual intercourse.

Mrs. Hill is trapped between the felt desire of an acquired self and the unarticulated needs of an inner self. More often than not, she falls into the sphere bounded by her acquired self: "She [Mrs. Hill] respected school teachers as a class but despised them as individuals. At the same time, she needed to believe in their infallibility. Otherwise she could not attempt to copy the clothes they wore, the way they fixed their hair or the way they spoke—or the authority with which they were able to confront and dominate less well educated men" (Walker, 187). Mrs. Hill is not capable of providing her daughter with an Afro-American historical perspective because she is more interested in bourgeois precedent than in historically based social change; indeed, she is satisfied with the current arrangement between blacks and whites. Her goal is to obtain peace and a method for moving through life. Because her perspective is not derived from the history of her own people, it is impossible for her to attain peace of mind. Mrs. Hill is surprised by Meridian's actions because she does not know her daughter, a situation guaranteed to result in problems.

In an effort to still the tension resulting from the warring expressions of the acquired and inner selves, Mrs. Hill plays the role of martyr. "Blame me for trusting you" is what she says when Meridian complains about her cryptic warning, "Be sweet. Don't be fast," when telling her daughter about sex. Meridian is impregnated by Eddie, and this furthers Mrs. Hill's martyrdom: "I have six children . . . though I never wanted to have any, and I raised them myself" (Walker, 90). Raising children is not a labor of love; it is simply labor: "In the ironing of her children's clothes she expended all the energy she might have openly put into loving them" (Walker, 79).

Discovering a real-life parallel to match the childhood of the fictional Meridian is less important than realizing that her mother's bourgeois mentality was common among blacks during the era of the civil rights movement. The stereotypical view regarding the privileges of class affiliation—teachers were the only professionals in the community, the bringers of culture, the trend setters—was common in the South during the period that provides the historical context for *Meridian.* An example of the exalted position teachers occupied follows. The circumstances concern a civil rights march in Selma, Alabama: "F. D. Reese led one hundred and twenty-five black teachers from Brown Chapel to the courthouse, where he and they were prodded and pushed by the club-toting sheriff—while the television cameras of NBC captured it all for the nation. The teachers had been holding back, watching with apprehension and misgivings. In those days school teachers were the upper class among blacks in the South, the only professionals of their race in the Black Belt counties" (Webb and Nelson, 33–34). Although the above example illustrates a progressive trait of black educators that is not apparent in the thinking of Mrs. Hill, it also serves to illustrate the high regard in which black teachers were held. The perception of authority implicit in assigning black teachers to an "upper class" indicates that many southern blacks had the same class prejudices as did whites. For blacks, such a perception can be debilitating because it interferes with social change. To be sure, in most struggles for social change, the rebelling group sheds the perspectives of the dominating group so as to define change from the perspective of its own history. The teachers involved in the civil rights movement had begun the process of defining themselves from the perspective of their own history and needs. The exalted positions given teachers was similar to Mrs. Hill's perspective, and it is similar to the one that dominated during the era of the civil rights movement.

An early SNCC member makes a similar point in indicating how the goals of his generation differed from those of his parent's generation:

> Our parents had the NAACP. Its practice of pursuing "test cases" through the courts and using laws and the Constitution to fight racial discrimination was suited to their temperaments. We needed something more. As far as we were concerned, the NAACP's approach was too slow, too courteous, too deferential and too ineffectual.
>
> In thousands of instances parents, frightened of reprisals, tried to get their children to quit demonstrating. For the most part, they were unsuccessful. The Negro college students leading the demonstrations and the

thousands of non-students assisting them were responding to something that transcended parent-child relationships. (Sellers, 19)

History demands an alteration in methods and goals.

Mr. Hill is a sensitive man, given to weeping over injustices heaped on native Americans. Meridian sneaks into her father's study; the walls are covered with "photographs of Indians: Sitting Bull, Crazy Horse, Geronimo, Little Bear, Yellow Flower and a drawing of Minnehaha and Hiawatha." He notices the intruder: "Her father looked up from his map, his face was wet with tears, which she mistook, for a moment, for sweat. Shocked and frightened, she ran away" (Walker, 53). Although Meridian and her father share a sensitivity to the sufferings of others, that sensitivity never becomes a basis for a father-daughter relationship capable of preparing Meridian for adulthood.

Her road into womanhood is paved by an unwanted pregnancy and marriage, neither of which she seems fully capable of understanding. For Meridian responds to all stimuli from the murky security of a semiconscious state.

After impregnating Meridian, Eddie does the proper thing by marrying her. The new bride and expectant mother does not make connections considered normal for a woman in her condition. A repentant Eddie, "burrowing his bristly head into her lap," asks, " 'Do you forgive me?' 'Forgive you for what?' It had not occurred to her to blame him. She felt, being pregnant, almost as if she'd contracted a communicable disease, that the germs had been in the air and that her catching the disease was no one's fault" (Walker, 62). Having bourgeois standards, despite the absence of the opportunity or the ability to realize those standards, makes Eddie a "good boy." He draws a detailed picture of future comfort: " 'We'll have a house like Mr. Yateson. It will have cactus plants around it and a sky blue driveway and painted blue trim. In the dining room there'll be a chandelier like the ones in Joan Crawford movies. And there'll be carpeting wall to wall and all the rooms will be different colors' " (Walker, 64). " 'Um-hum,' she would nod vaguely at Eddie's dream." He remains well-mannered throughout their brief marriage. His complaints are basic: " 'And tonight, please, open your legs all the way,' " he says to the pregnant Meridian as he began "his assault from her left side." Meridian could have tolerated these demands were it not for her growing realization that Eddie would always be a boy, forever "fetching and carrying and courteously awaiting orders from someone above" (Walker, 70). She criticizes her manchild and he, unaware of any possible fault resting in his comfortable pursuit of symbols (he told Meridian once that he was not interested in education but in finishing school), slowly drifts away: "A night here, three or four days absent there, and with a cooling off, slightly, of his usual affections to the boy" (Walker, 71). He leaves his wife and son. "She [Meridian] was still only seventeen. A drop-out from high school, a deserted wife, a mother" (Walker, 75–76). Meridian's problems are largely the result of her directionless upbringing.

For Meridian, history assumes the catalytic role that is usually assigned to parents and friends, and as a consequence her world changes:

> On the day he [Eddie] left, she had walked past a house not far from hers, where—since it was early summer—all doors and windows were open. People, young and old, her own age, were everywhere. They milled about inside, shouted out of windows, to those outside, looked carefree (as childless young people her own age, always now looked to her) and yet as if sensitive to some outside surveilance beyond her own staring. But she was the only person on the street. And she stopped to look only because it was a black family's house and there were several young white people. (Walker, 72)

Meridian awoke the next morning to find the same house featured in a television news story—it was shown as it looked before being fire-bombed. Three children as well as some of the young people who were guarding the house were killed. That the young people anticipated trouble and that trouble occurred amazed Meridian; their knowing intimated a consciousness foreign to her: "And so it was that one day in the middle of April in 1960 Meridian became aware of the past and present of the larger world" (Walker, 73).

The initial foray into activism on the part of various civil rights activists was not, I am sure, as dramatic as Meridian's. But consciousness-changing events occurred which made it impossible for such people to see the world as they had before (Sellers, 3–32). In other instances, individuals were slowly drawn into the movement without knowing why (Webb and Nelson).

"A month after the bombing Meridian walked through the gate of a house and knocked on the door. 'I've come to volunteer,' she said"

(Walker, 80). Her volunteering is a semiconscious act; she is not aware of the confluence of her innate curiosity and sensitivity and the objective reality of her social status—for she remains a deserted mother and a high school dropout. She has no clear information about what it is she is volunteering for or any particular skills to offer. People are, of course, attracted to political causes for reasons other than the goals of those causes, and Meridian falls in this category. She is introduced to Swinbourne and Truman and spends her first day pecking at the typewriter. "After an hour she was able to lay out a perfect copy of the petition, except that she'd put an 'e' on Negro" (Walker, 182).

Without direction Meridian is sucked into the most strong and positive movement of her time, just as some white students first moved into SNCC. Jane Stembridge, a white student who joined SNCC, says of her initial meeting: " 'The most inspiring moment for me was the first time I heard the students sing "We Shall Overcome." . . . It was hot that night upstairs in the auditorium. Students had just come in from all over the South. . . . I had just driven down from Union Seminary in New York—out of it, except that I cared, and that I was a Southerner. . . . It was inspiring because it was the beginning, and because, in a sense, it was the purest moment. I am a romantic. But I call this moment the one' " (Zinn, 33). Emotion served as the primary impetus for involvement among many activists. They did not come to the movement with clear ideas about social change; they simply felt that something was wrong in the way Afro-Americans were treated and they wanted to do something to change it. The challenge such activists faced is the same one that Meridian faces: after the exhilaration of the initial involvement they must discover themselves in the context of history. This last imperative is so important because its absence increases the chances that activism will be reduced to a spontaneous response to all events, and it also heightens the chance that people will repeat the mistakes of previous generations.

Meridian's clerical work quickly gives way to intense political involvement and police repression. Brutality is an objective condition that brings Meridian and Truman closer together: "When the sheriff grabbed her by the hair and someone else began punching her and kicking her in the back, she did not even scream, except very intensely in her own mind, and the scream of Truman's name. And what she meant by it was not even that she was in love with him: what she meant by it was that they were at a time and place in History that forced the trivial to fall away—and they were absolutely together" (Walker, 84). The brutality forces "the trivial to fall away," but there is no political consciousness to delineate issues beyond obvious repression. Meridian starts as a volunteer typist and quickly becomes a demonstrator; she spends little time studying the goals of the civil rights movement or contemplating the meaning of her involvement within the context of her personal history. This latter deficiency gives her political involvement a ritualistic character. A critical consciousness does not inform her activism, a problem common to some activists in the real world.

Cleve Sellers writes about a display of spontaneous activism that, at least for a time, went wild. After SNCC members attempted to enter the state capitol in Montgomery to deliver a petition and were refused, they camped on the spot and began a vigil. Because of bad weather, they decided to adjourn to the First Baptist Church; they later moved to the Dexter Avenue Baptist Church, still with the intent of continuing their vigil. Without checking with the members inside the church, James Forman issued a national call for relief for the students, and some hours later a huge truck pulled up to the church and dumped an array of camping equipment on the pavement. The police sent James Bevel of the Southern Christian Leadership Conference in to negotiate with the students in an effort to get them to leave the church. Sellers writes: "After much discussion of the student vigil, we [SNCC] decided that it could be used to draw attention away from Selma. . . . Although there was a tremendous amount of pressure on the students—the church's officials had turned off the water, heat and electricity—and we were confident that they could hold out until we mobilized support. Stokely was inside with them" (Sellers, 126). The student vigil had assumed a high degree of symbolic significance. It was intended to show that the students were determined not to be disbanded before they delivered their petition. One key to success depended on the students remaining where they were. Sellers writes:

> Although it was early, the figure approaching me was unmistakable. It was Stokely. Rushing toward him, I began firing questions.
>
> "What in the hell are you doing out here? Why in the hell aren't you in the church with the students? Where are the students? What in the hell is going on in this goddamn town anyway? Why did you leave the church?"

> I was so upset that I didn't immediately notice that Stokely was acting strangely. After a moment, when I realized that he wasn't responding to my questions, I calmed down and looked at him closely. There were large tears rolling down his cheeks. He didn't know where he was. The tension, frustration and fatigue had proven too much. He had freaked out completely. (Sellers, 127)

A protest that began as an attempt to deliver a petition to the state capitol turned into a strange vigil, the symbolic significance of which seemed to have increased with each passing moment. The absence of clear plans made it necessary to make each move as it came. The attempt to act before devising an overall strategy was often problematic. Despite these shortcomings, activists continued to struggle to make America live up to her promise of equality.

In *Meridian,* the physical ramifications of political involvement are profound: "She was always in a state of constant tears, so that she could do whatever she was doing—canvassing, talking at rallies, tying her sneakers, laughing—while tears rolled slowly and ceaselessly down her cheeks. This might go on for days. Then, suddenly, it would stop, and some other symptom would appear. The shaking of her hands, or the twitch in her left eye" (Walker, 84–85) These physical symptoms foreshadow Meridian's periodic paralysis. The problems, however, do not move Meridian any closer to full consciousness, to the merging of personal history and political involvement. At one point, she goes to the spigot to wet her blouse to wipe tear gas from Truman's eyes. When she returns, Truman is gone: "A police car was seen careening down the street. She stood in the street feeling the cool wet spot on her side, wondering what to do" (Walker, 85). Well she might wonder: the nature of her involvement, though infinitely broader in implication and outlook than was her earlier circumscribed existence, has the character of the novice's initial foray into the widening world of the unknown. The surprise and confusion that Meridian experiences were paralleled by some civil rights activists. Specifically, there was a clear relationship between historical literacy and the ability of individuals to adjust when something unexpected happened (Sellers). Again, historical literacy is determined by an individual discovering him or herself in the context of Afro-American history.

But Meridian is not stuck in her hometown. At eighteen she is awarded a scholarship: "A generous (and wealthy) white family in

Connecticut who wished to help some of the poor, courageous blacks they saw marching and getting their heads whipped nightly on TV—decided, as a gesture of their liberality and concern, to send a smart black girl to Saxon College in Atlanta, a school this family had endowed for three generations" (Walker, 86). Going to Saxon means putting her son up for adoption. Anticipating her mother's response, Meridian brings several friends along for moral support. " 'No matter what your mother says,' Delores continued, 'just remember she spends her time making prayer pillows.' " Speaking with Christian clarity, Mrs. Hall says: " 'Well, it can't be normal. . . . It can't be right to give away your child.' " Meridian responds: " 'But this is the only chance I have, Mama' " (Walker, 87). Mrs. Hill will not understand: " 'You should *want* Eddie, Jr. . . . Unless you're some kind of monster. And no daughter of mine is a monster, surely' " (Walker, 89). The circle of her logic complete, Mrs. Hill embellishes her correctness with continued references to Christian morality which make Meridian feel guilty. Despite feelings of guilt, Meridian accepts the scholarship.

Once on campus, her decision haunts her: "For she began hearing a voice when she studied for exams, and when she walked about the academic halls, and when she looked from her third floor dormitory window. A voice cursed her existence—an existence that could not live up to the standard of motherhood that had gone before" (Walker, 91). The determined scholar plunges on: "She was not to pause long enough to respond to this spiritual degeneration . . . until she was in her second year" (Walker, 93).

Saxon College wants its women to know and practice the "proper values" to maximize chances for social acceptance in white America. The school's preoccupation with molding young black women into "ladies" obviates political involvement, causing Saxon women to feel as though "they had two enemies: Saxon . . . and the larger, more deadly enemy, white racist society" (Walker, 95).

In its attention to genteel precedent, the school is similar to Mrs. Hill, who is equally apolitical: " 'It never bothered me to sit in the back of the bus, you get just as good a view and you don't have all those nasty white asses passing you' " (Walker, 85). The school's emphasis on purity and correctness contradicts Meridian's personal history; the mother and former wife feels herself "to be flying under false colors as an 'innocent' Saxon student." The contradiction affects the way she views her political involvement: "The scenes she personally witnessed in the Atlanta streets, combined with this [Saxon's attempt to create "ladies"] caused the majority of her waking moments to seem fragmented, surreal" (Walker, 96). Her political involvement will be coherent when her past becomes meaningful in the context of that involvement.

Again, this tendency existed among many Afro-American activists in the real world. The confusion they sometimes felt was a result of their personal history. Their actions were not always a result of well-planned tactics but a response to one imperative or another. Early in the civil rights movement, many of the student organizations often reacted spontaneously and without an overall plan, which is understandable in light of the attention the movement enjoyed in the media. Early civil rights activists may have assumed that the nation was in agreement with their goals and that all they needed to do was to point out the contradiction between the promise of America and the reality of racism. In any case, they saw no need for deep thinking to locate themselves in the context of Afro-American history. To paraphrase Julian Bond, the struggle was about hamburgers.

Because Meridian loves Truman, if he returns her love, he will be able to help her bridge her worlds of personal history and political involvement. For the two have yet to come together in a conscious and meaningful fashion. Truman, however, is too self-consumed and presumptuous to be useful. In fact, the way Truman introduces himself to Meridian foreshadows the ease with which he is ultimately able to abandon political activism. *"Je m'appele* Truman Held," he tells the unsophisticated Meridian, who marvels at his handsomeness and apparent worldliness. Once he and Meridian establish a relationship, he continues to season each conversation with French: "He believed profoundly that anything said in French sounded better and he also believed that people who spoke French were better than people (Les Miserables!) who did not" (Walker, 100). He whispers to Meridian, "en français of course," 'I am so glad you came to Saxon.' " Although the emphasis on self-definition and a conscious infusion of Afro-American culture with a pre-Arab and pre-European African sensibility is more a part of the black power than the civil rights movement, Truman's French nationalism is incorrect in that it reflects a world-view that alienates him from the black people he wants to help.

Truman is not able to help Meridian bridge her worlds because he is too confused. Unlike Meridian, though, he projects an image of being in control. He is a jumble of impulses without a synthesizing and directing consciousness. Having seen him as the "Conquering Prince," Meridian is eventually hurt badly by his careless escapades into boundless possibility which lacks a historical base. He sees no relationship between his desires and history: "He was startled by the coolness with which she received his assertion that what he had decided, after considering '*le maitre*' was that if he dated white girls it must be, essentially, a matter of sex. She laughed when she saw he expected her to be pleased and reassured, a bitter laugh that sent him away again, his chin thrust forward against her misunderstanding" (Walker, 106). A childhood of debilitating neglect is compounded by a lover who is insensitive to her most basic needs. In his reduction of white women to sexual tools, he still manages to elevate them to a plateau higher than the one afforded Meridian and other black women. By razing the idol of white womanhood, he reinforces it, and by idolizing black womanhood, he undercuts it. For Meridian's political involvement to be meaningful, she must acknowledge both the strengths and weaknesses of her past. Truman's simple idealism and selfishness do not help Meridian in this task.

Truman is true to his word. He dates white women and is consequently blinded to any interracial problems that black and white women civil rights activists might have. Meridian relates an episode in which she and a white exchange student attempt to register Mrs. Turner, an elderly black woman. Mrs. Turner invites the pair in and gives them dinner: " 'I wants to feed y'all real good, 'cause I don't believe in votin'. The good lord he takes care of most of my problems. You know he heal the sick and race the dead. Comfort the uncomfortable and blesses the meek' " (Walker, 102). Meridian knows immediately that logic will not persuade Mrs. Turner to vote. That decision must come from the special logic of her religious concerns. Lynne Rabinowitz, the white exchange student, is unimpressed by Mrs. Turner's assessment of social change: "So God fixes the road in front of your house, does he? . . . Jesus Christ must be pleased to let you live in a house like this." Lynne is moved by her own lucidity and continues. She is hot: "The good lord must get his jollies every time you have to hop outside to that toilet in the rain. The Holy Ghost must rejoice when your children catch pneumonia every winter."

Meridian decides that Mrs. Turner is "beyond the boundaries of politics" (Walker, 102).

Truman is clearly unimpressed with Mrs. Turner and calls her *"La fanatique."* This episode indicates Meridian's sensitivity to the people she desires to help and illustrates Truman's blithe arrogance. He is more like Lynne Rabinowitz than Meridian. He will win the blacks over with a brand of logic that, if accepted, would undercut any systems of belief and logic that have maintained them over the years. These activists must learn that people can be changed only when their belief systems are accorded respect; bludgeoning logic alone is an insufficient tool for political change.

Truman's feelings about white women are further illustrated by his response to Meridian's telling of several black women's reaction to white exchange students snapping photos of "the girls straightening their hair and also of them coming out of the showers." Charlene, one of the black photo subjects, threatens to beat the photographers if the film is not destroyed: "This here ain't New Guinea," she tells them. Truman is understanding of the white students: "They were just curious about *les noirs* . . . when I was in Paris I was curious about the French. I'm sure I did some strange things, too." Unmoved, Meridian asks, "Like photographing them while they styled their hair and when they emerged from the shower? Or is it true that the French never bathe?" (Walker, 103). To Truman, black women have no legitimate right to complain about a form of behavior—curiosity— that is universal. By universalizing the black women's complaint through the French comparison, he denies that complaint its historical meaning. The relationship between black and white women in America has been less than harmonious, especially during the civil rights movement.

In the novel, Meridian asks Truman what he sees in the white girls he dates. He responds, "They read the *New York Times*" (Walker, 143). Truman's arrogance aside, Meridian's question is echoed in the feelings of some black women who were involved in the early phases of the civil rights movement: "The Negro's antagonism [toward white civil rights workers] is further aggravated by sexual conflicts. . . . Negro women, oppressed by the value society has placed on having white skin, regard the white workers as an 'unfair competition.' 'I think,' one Negro girl told Poussaint angrily, 'all these white girls down here sat up North dreaming about being raped . . . and

came down here to see what is was like' " ("African Queen Complex,"
23). Although Meridian does not state her feelings in just this way, it
is clear that they are similar to those of the black woman quoted
above. All of this history misses Truman as he marches merrily to his
own ahistorical tune.

Truman eventually marries Lynne Rabinowitz. He never clar-
ifies his motives for marrying Lynne, but through the courtship and
marriage, he ceases political activism. Even Lynne tells him at one
point that for him she is an oddity to be periodically exhibited. She is
capable, however, of more direct comment: " 'You only married me
because you were too much of a coward to throw a bomb at all the
crackers who make you sick. You're like the rest of these nigger
zombies. No life of your own at all unless it's something against white
folks.' " She ultimately condemns Truman for "running off as soon as
black became beautiful" (Walker, 149).

Lynne's last comment is continuous with a part of the sixties
when interracial relationships were not in vogue. The condemnations
were a part of the Afro-American creative outburst labeled the black
arts movement (Jones and Neal), in which white was incarnate of evil.
There were real-life condemnations and conversions. Of the latter
group, LeRoi Jones's metamorphosis into Amiri Baraka was the most
spectacular. So Lynne's charge against Truman for running away has
many historical antecedents.

Truman is much more motivated by ideas than by feelings, and
as a result his relationships are thin, lacking the substance of emotion.
Black and white women for him are stereotypes, but even here the
black woman loses out to her white counterpart. For him, white
women represent culture and sophistication (they do, after all, read
the *New York Times*) and black women represent sensuality and
intuition. As one might expect, these stereotypes have clear analogies
in the popular culture. Eldridge Cleaver's admission that he practiced
raping black women to perfect his technique before raping white
women (Cleaver, 26) and Stokely Carmichael's assertion that the
prone position was the only one for black women represent these
stereotypes. Cleaver, operating within the white male tradition of
using the black woman for sexual practice and experimentation,
would not even accord her the lowly status of an object of lust. She is
only a stand-in, an animated corpse for cold experimentation. Carmichael would, I suppose, have the black woman a live sperm re-

pository. Although Truman does not elaborate upon these stereotypes when he attempts to explain his actions, they clearly direct him.

The challenge for Truman is to reclaim his past in such a way that he can make sense of his activism, attain some peace, and then move on with his life. His mistake in this repsect is to assume that the answers to his problems lie neatly packaged in Meridian. He seeks her out and tries to explain why they never married and why he needs her:

> [Truman] "I don't owe Lynne the way I do you. You notice I didn't lie and say I don't love her at all. She meant a great deal to me. But you're different. Loving you is different—"
> [Meridian] "Because I'm black?"
> [Truman] "You make me feel healthy, purposeful—"
> [Meridian] "Because I'm black?"
> [Truman] "Because you're you, damn it! The woman I should have married and didn't!"
> [Meridian] "Should have loved and didn't." (Walker, 140)

This conversation proves Lynne right in condemning Truman for his new black consciousness. Truman is willing to forget or deemphasize the insensitivity he showed Meridian during their time together. Nor does he know, however, that he impregnated Meridian and that she had an abortion.

Truman must confront his past insensitivity and ignorance and, in a sense, do penance. In this Meridian has no active role; she may suggest and remind, but it is Truman who must stitch his ragged life together. On one of his visits to Meridian, who remains in the South, he tries to explain himself:

> [Truman] "I grieve in a different way. . . . "
> [Meridian] "I know. . . . "
> [Truman] "What do you know?"
> [Meridian] "I know you grieve by running away.
> By pretending you were never there."
> [Truman] "When things are finished it is best to leave."
> [Meridian] "And pretend they were never started?"
> [Truman] "Yes."
> [Meridian] "But that's not possible." (Walker 27)

Truman attempts the impossible and does not succeed. The psychic damage resulting from the explosions that political activism set off must be dealt with. In the world when this does not happen, the actions of activists become hard for their peers to understand.

For Truman, the answer to these problems lies with black people. And in this, Meridian can be helpful. She helps him learn patience and respect for black people. The two attempt to get an elderly black man to vote:

> [The Man] "What good is the vote, if we don't own nothing?"
>
> [Truman] "Do you want free medicine for your wife? A hospital that'll take black people through the front door? A good school for Johnny, Jr. and a job no one can take away?"
>
> [The Man] "You know I do. . . . "
>
> [Truman] "Well, voting probably won't get it for you, not in your life time. . . . "
>
> [The Man] "What will it get me but a lot of trouble. . . ?"
>
> [Truman] "I don't know. . . . It may be useless. Or maybe it can be the beginning of your voice. . . . You start on simple things and move on. . . . "
>
> [The Man] "No. . . . I don't have time for foolishness. My wife is dying. My boy don't have no shoes. Go somewhere else and find somebody that ain't got to work all the time for pennies, like I do."
>
> [Meridian] "Okay!" (Walker, 204–5)

Meridian and Truman later return with a bag of groceries. The man peeks into the bag, saying, " 'I ain't changed my mind.' . . . And they did not see him again until the Monday after Mother's day, when he brought six rabbits already skinned and ten newspaper logs; and under the words WILL YOU BE BRAVE ENOUGH TO VOTE in Meridian's yellow pad, he wrote his name in large black letters" (Walker, 205). Truman's flippancy is not apparent here because he has learned to accept black people who think and act differently than he does. There is no need to be strident. He slowly begins to understand Meridian. More important, he sees that he will have to enter the cocoon of black folk culture to find that which his earlier presumptuousness precluded. Meridian leaves, suggesting that Truman stay in her house to begin his rebirth. "He climbed shakingly into Meridian's sleeping bag." The confused revolutionary must be reborn.

The relationship between Truman and Meridian illustrates one dimension of relationships within the civil rights movement. We see the devastating effect the activism can have on relationships when the participants have not clarified the nature of their involvement. The struggle inherent to social change creates a vacuum that makes all things possible. For individuals like Truman, it is easy to substitute personal desires for political imperatives. As Lynne notes, it is easier for Truman to marry her than to throw a molotov cocktail. The vacuum that social change creates also works to separate Truman from his roots in the black community. The church and the folkways of average black men and women are institutions that do not initially direct Truman's actions. He is more French than Afro-American.

As a consequence of having separated himself from these institutions, Truman is unable to relate to Meridian. Because he is floating in a curious no-man's-land of colorless bliss, Meridian can be at best only an idea to him. The absence of historical literacy damns any possible relationship the two might have. The novel ends with Truman beginning the process of rejuvenation that Meridian has already completed.

Meridian's decision to go south at a time when interest in the civil rights movement had bottomed out, when, indeed, others were busying themselves in an effort to fit into whatever niches America might make available, is continuous with her healthy respect for black people: "Meridian alone was holding onto something the others had let go. If not completely, then partially—by their words today, their deeds tomorrow. But what none of them seemed to understand was that she felt herself to be, not holding on to something from the past, but *held* by something in the past: by the memory of old black men in the South who, caught by surprise in the eye of the camera, never shifted their position but looked directly back; by the sight of young girls singing in a country choir" (Walker, 27–28). Meridian is immersed in black folk culture and therefore finds the latest political abstractions of her peers unworkable. They want to know if she can kill for the revolution. " 'Maybe I could sort of grow into the idea of killing other human beings.' " This is not enough for Anne-Marion and her other friends: " 'But can you say you probably will? That you will kill?' " Meridian is honest: she says no. This exchange takes place in New York, some years after her aborted Saxon experience, and it reflects the growing rhetoric of the black power movement. For Meridian, questions remain about her personal history that political involvement has exacerbated—questions that must be answered if her life is to be coherent and meaningful. Her ability to say no to the questions of her revolutionary friends indicates that she is more fully conscious of herself as an individual involved in political struggle than she was during the civil rights movement, when she lapsed into periodic states of not knowing. She marvels at her friends' questions and wonders: "If they committed murder—and to her even revolutionary murder was murder—what would the music be like?" (Walker, 28). She finally tells her friends, " 'I'll go back to the people, live among them, like Civil Rights workers used to do' " (Walker, 31).

Meridian's actions in the South are similar to the semiconscious martyrdom that characterizes her mother's life. She sacrifices her physical self on the altar of political understanding whereas Mrs. Hill's sacrifice is ostensibly for her children. The only clear goal that mother and daughter have is peace of mind. Meridian's martyrdom borders on masochism; she is emaciated; her hair is falling out; and she has attacks of paralysis. These problems result from neglect, but the neglect does not bring peace of mind. Thus her time in the South seems initially like some odd penance, a cleansing that past shortcomings require her to make.

A traveling carnival in Chicokema allows blacks to visit its vaunted "freak show" only on Thursdays. This injustice becomes a cause for Meridian; she leads a band of young blacks into the show, but not before two of the townspeople start a tank purchased to quell race riots. Meridian marches up to the tank, raps sharply on its hull, and beckons the encased heroes to emerge. The struggle, even when the goals are suspect, must go on. Indeed, it goes on even when the principles lack focus. She explains her actions to the visiting Truman: "'They [the black children] said she [the freak] was made of plastic and were glad they hadn't waited till Thursday when they would have to pay money to see her. Besides, it was a hot day. They were bored. There was nothing else to do' " (Walker, 26). So the struggle becomes a pastime, a picnic to be spontaneously enacted when other diversions have failed.

Meridian remains sincere in her activism, but the lack of a synthesizing tradition that can envelop her past, her political involvement, and the resulting tensions between the two makes her return to the south a random affair. She moves from town to town, teaching in one, doing odd jobs in another. For Meridian, however, peace of mind and purpose reside in the folkways and institutions of the South. Out of no particular passion, she turns to the black church: "Sometime after the spring of '68, Meridian began going irregularly to church" (Walker, 193). Her attendance at a particular black church draws the various impulses of her life together. She is shocked first by the prayer, then by the music, and finally by the sermon. Each element in the service has a political dimension that is new to Meridian. The songs have a "quite martial melody" and are "oddly death defying." She is drawn into the song and finds herself quoting Margaret Walker: "Let the martial songs be written . . . let the dirges disappear" (Walker, 195). The sermon is lucid and political: "Then the preacher launched into an attack on President Nixon, whom he called "Tricky Dick!" He looked down on the young men in the audience and forbade them to participate in the Vietnam war. He told the young women to stop looking for husbands and try to get something useful in their heads. He told the older congregants that they should be ashamed of the way they had their young children fight their battles for them" (Walker, 195). The preacher's condemnations and exhortations continue, but it is finally the way they are delivered that Meridian notices.

"It struck Meridian that he was deliberately imitating King, that he and all his congregation knew he was consciously keeping that voice alive. It was like a *play*" (Walker, 196). The play is more than good theater; it regenerates a tradition capable of rousing its inhabitants to action. Although the black church brings Meridian home, she realizes that she cannot kill for the revolution. In a brutal aside as to the actions of "revolutionary" Anne-Marion and her friends, Walker writes: "She [Meridian] had heard of nothing revolutionary this group had done, since she left them ten summers ago. Anne-Marion, she knew, had become a well-known poet whose poems were about her two children, and the quality of the light that fell across a lake she owned" (Walker, 201). This assessment carries with it the signifying character that is typical of the revolutionary who is disappointed by a friend's decision to return to the establishment. The criticism of Anne-Marion and her friends is characteristic of the historical period that provides the novel's context in which people made assertions concerning their commitment to the "struggle" or to the "revolution."

Actually at the root of the rhetoric was one basic question: who is the blackest? No definitive answer was found because none existed. Despite the failure of her friends to do anything revolutionary,

Meridian still feels that she will "not belong to the future. I am to be left, listening to the old music, beside the highway" (Walker, 201). This thought barely takes hold when Meridian, perhaps remembering the play enacted in church, realizes that "it is the song of the people, transformed by the experiences of each generation, that holds them together, and if any part of it is lost the people suffer and are without soul. If I can only do that, my role will not have been a useless one after all" (Walker, 201).

The divorced wife who allows her son to be raised by strangers, the high school dropout turned activist, the guilt-ridden coed who must have an abortion because her "Conquering Prince" proves less than loving, the near vagabond who practices civil rights (rites) rituals in various small towns is finally whole. She has a purpose in life.

A failure to confront contradictions in one's personal history, especially when those contradictions are exacerbated by political activism, causes problems for characters in *Meridian*. For Meridian, the problems are evidenced in physical degeneration and near madness. The vehicle that suggests a continous thread to stitch her disparate life together is the black church. A precedent for radical love exists. She will keep the voice of the people alive and soothe the warriors with her song. Meridian becomes a modern-day griot. For Truman, failure to deal with personal history sends him on periodic forays into the South in search of Meridian.

Like the novels previously discussed, *Meridian* suggests that the interplay between personal history and political activism cannot be ignored, nor can it be smoothed over by slogans. The vacuum created by tensions resulting from this contradiction is filled by racial history. For Meridian the answer is the black church. For Truman the answer has not emerged, though he has begun the process. Because Meridian asserts that precedents exist in the racial past, the instructive imperative is clear.

References

"African Queen Complex." *Newsweek*, 23 May 1966, p. 23.
Cabral, Amilcar. *Revolution in Guinea: Selected Texts*. New York: Monthly Review Press, 1969.

Cleaver, Eldridge. *Soul on Ice.* New York: Dell, 1968.

Fanon, Frantz. *The Wretched of the Earth.* New York: Grove Press, 1961.

Giddings, Paula. *When and Where I Enter: The Impact of Black Women on Race and Sex in America.* Morrow, 1984.

Jones, LeRoi, and Larry Neal, eds. *Black Fire.* New York: Morrow, 1968.

Karenga, Maulana. "Overturning Ourselves: From Mystification to Meaningful Struggle." *Black Scholar,* October 1972, pp. 6–14.

Marable, Manning. *Blackwater: Historical Studies in Race, Class Consciousness, and Revolution.* Dayton, Ohio: Black Praxis Press, 1981.

Sellers, Cleve. *River of No Return.* New York: Morrow, 1973.

Walker, Alice. *Meridian.* New York: Harcourt Brace Jovanovitch, 1976.

Webb, Sheyann, and Rachel West Nelson. *Selma, Lord Selma.* University, Ala.: University of Alabama Press, 1980.

Zinn, Howard. *SNCC: The New Abolitionists.* Boston: Beacon Press, 1964.

7

Look What They Done to My Song:
New Music for the Black Church

The events that provide the historical context for *Look What They Done to My Song* deal with the transition from the civil rights movement to the black power movement. The shift is illustrated by the central character, Mack. His internal conflict results from the propensity of Afro-Americans to betray each other, and it is in the handling of this conflict that we see the transition from the civil rights movement to the black power movement. In Mack's initial perception of social conflict and reality he almost passively assumes that some form of integration might provide the solution. As he grows in knowledge of himself and of his people—a process of acquiring freedom and literacy—he sees himself as a central force in infusing African and Afro-American history into the institution that is presented as being capable of nurturing the consciousness necessary to social change—the black church. In its adherence to self-reliance and its assumption that answers to individual and racial conflicts lie in the racial past, Mack's new perspective is similar to that found among characters in the black power novels and among black power advocates in the real world.

More generally, the shift from the civil rights movement to the black power movement is tied to the attempts of Afro-Americans to live full, self-conscious lives in the context of an alien and capitalist Euro-American culture that routinely brutalizes Afro-Americans through an intricate network of policing forces. The novel illustrates the centrality of freedom and literacy to conflict resolution, particularly when those conflicts result from intraracial strife.

But all of this is not immediately apparent. Indeed, read superficially, *Look What They Done to My Song* is a novel about the attempts of a musician and his friend to find suitable employment—employment that allows Mack the musician to blow "unity music" through his tenor saxophone and Ubangi, a small-time entrepreneur, to move his shady ventures into the "big time" without losing control of them. They are seeking literacy, that special fusion of vocation and spirit which comes with historical understanding. The environment in which both characters function gets in the way of their obtaining literacy. Euro-America is not interested in creating historically conscious black men and women.

Although Mack and Ubangi, the major characters, assume that geographical change will advance their quest for literacy, actually they can achieve such literacy only within themselves and within Afro-American history. The bulk of the novel, however, illustrates the consequences of black life in capitalist America and provides the context for understanding intraracial conflict in America.

We meet Jesse Dawkins, Ova Easy, Crackerjack, and an array of other mediocre "pimps" who employ lies, disguises, and bad faith in their acquisitive quests. Like the smoothest confidence man, these characters can sell the Brooklyn Bridge every five minutes without ever changing expressions. Jesse Dawkins, a black police officer, offers to release Mack from prison for a small fee. When Dawkins learns that Mack has only one dollar and twenty-one cents, he gladly accepts it on the promise of future payment commensurate with the services rendered. A grateful Mack bounds from his cell, only to discover that his woman friend has already posted bail. Ova Easy is a wiry prostitute who is made available to Ubangi by a "friend" at a "pimp's convention." Ubangi does not check out his gift and belatedly discovers that Ova Easy is actually a man, who apparently works for the police. Although Ubangi's futile schemes are exploitive, in attempting to carry them out, he is so naive and inept as to be benign and laughably pathetic.

These characters are illiterate, operating without historical knowledge. Their good traits are distorted by Euro-American culture because that culture, though penetrated with various Afro-Americanisms, is not a true expression of their history; yet they must respond to and operate in the context of the problems and opportunities posed by Euro-American culture. Their deformity is alleviated as they discover themselves within the context of Afro-American history.

In addition to the economic constraints the characters face are policing forces whose periodic forays into the black community are lawless and devastating. Wendell, a black actor, is mistaken by the "Mafioso" for a nationalist leader and is gunned down. A black club owner is found with a bullet in his skull. The normal affronts by the police continue: their most recent "mistake" is the shooting of a ten-year-old boy. The policing forces, like the economic forces, function to limit black potential. Although these social forces are not capable of destroying black desires for unity and greater community control, they do help to create and widen the gaps among black community members.

Mack wants to fill the multiplying gaps within the black community with his music. Music, his vocation, must find institutional expression if its spirit—which is one of unification and harmony—is to be realized. His club dates are not sufficient. The men and women who frequent the clubs at which he plays seek withdrawal as they slouch in corners or sit bent on stools at darkened bars. Even when the music inspires them, they move only to shake off responsibility. Dance is exorcism, releasing pent-up emotions, which, because of the pedestrian quality of these people's lives, will accumulate again during the week. The weekend comes and the ritual resumes. Because exceptions are rare, Mack realizes that he must play his music in another setting for it to have full expression. The proper setting is Crumbly Rock Baptist Church: its traditions are fluid enough not to be violated by accepting Mack's unity music.

When read more deeply, *Look What They Done to My Song* illustrates moments of discovery in Mack's life: he must respond to divisions within the black community that result from intraracial betrayal and the constraining nature of economic and policing forces. His hesitancy to respond forthrightly to these events—a hesitancy that is evidenced in constant though halfhearted participation in Ubangi's ventures, his unsatisfactory club dates, and his casual relationships with several women—is best understood as an attempt to forestall his destiny. A series of dramatic events move him to that confrontation. Malcolm X's assassination is the genesis, for it releases feelings that are too expansive for the New Mexico cultural/spiritual institutions available for expression. He moves slowly east, and through the people he meets and the roles they play in making him aware of himself and of how he fits into the framework of Afro-American history, that move becomes symbolic. For the East is a source of light, the beginning of a new day, and these meanings are precisely what Mack seeks. In succession he meets and is expanded and deepened by Reba and Dupree Sledge, Ubangi, Wendell, Antar, Novella Turner, and Reverend C. E. Fuller. Each contact moves Mack closer to himself, and by the end of the novel he is ready to act from his own set of imperatives. Because the events and relationships depicted in the novel occur in the context of a historical period characterized by attempts at cultural and political self-definition, what might otherwise be a limited *Bildungsroman* takes on broad significance: the problematic situations Mack confronts and ultimately solves become analogues to the situations confronted by Afro-American men and women who came to maturity during the late sixties and early seventies.

The novel's prologue consists of a historical and tightly structured monologue that foreshadows economic motivations for racial betrayal and the desire to mollify the betrayal's consequences through unconditional racial love. Mack is first the "juju priest to Shango" who uses "black magic" to transcend the results of "the first native betrayal when slaves . . . were exchanged for bracelets and rusty guns and the Bible." This is the public Mack, who is aware of the economic motivations for racial betrayal and also of a dominant consequence of that betrayal: "the blind curse that can put black hands to shredding black throats." The historical imperative is "to get back to that moment, to erase it, for the death and the pain even, but not the life and joy" (McCluskey, 4). Within the shattering contradiction of black complicity in slavery there lies some beauty.

A conflict between public responsibilities and private needs is suggested when Mack states that he is "black and human and must not deny his heart." Mack the individual has needs that might contradict his public responsibilities. Nevertheless, the public Mack remains "the sum of possibilities, lost, found . . . approaching." Mack's destiny is suggested: he is to help bridge different segments of the black community. Although aware of the contours of his destiny, Mack is slow to move because of the implicit conflict between public and private responsibilities. But because his personal conflict is not resolved through constant self-analysis—as are those of Ben in *Coming Home* and Ellington in *Tragic Magic*—he is best understood through his interactions with other characters, particularly from the point of view those other characters represent.

A stream-of-consciousness section halfway through the narrative functions as does the prologue to place Mack's actions within a social context. The wondering Mack is also reminded of his destiny. He chastises himself: "Right on time, you left home and blood and you flew. Thought that music could have a social good, could reveal unity among the group. Too early you have left town after town when the sun missed your front door" (McCluskey, 117). Mack concludes that once he he relaxes, his destiny will be attainable: "God will be your runnin' buddy, the way he's wanted to be all along, but you were running too fast" (McCluskey, 119). The partial serenity suggested by this observation is splintered when Martin Luther King, Jr., is assassinated. Speaking to a friend—still within the stream-of-consciousness framework—Mack reacts: "All of them must be killed. . . . All of them. With razors at close range, poison, with voodoo— anything, but they must die. . . . Spill their blood to remind them they are human too" (McCluskey, 121). As in the prologue ("I'm black, and human and must not deny my heart"), Mack's inner thoughts penetrate his public consciousness.

Early in the novel Mack reflects: "Word of Malcolm came from refugees pushing through town to L.A. I counted his death with that of so many others around the land as assassinations of spirit, a spirit whose only peace needed fury. I wanted to grow in that spirit and I guessed that growth needed the right place" (McCluskey, 7). Sante Fe, New Mexico, is not the "right place." Malcolm X's assassination ignites a fuse that sends Mack wandering eastward for a place to perfect his music. Columbus, Ohio, is the initial destination—a friend has written Mack, telling him of the need for a good tenor saxophonist—but the first sustained and meaningful contact is on the East Coast with an older black couple, Reba and Dupree Sledge, New Englanders who once lived in Lowndes County, Alabama.

These transported southerners maintain the cordiality and manners associated with that region. Indeed, their smooth and patient caring toward Mack makes them resemble blacks in the South who allowed black and white civil rights workers to stay in their homes

(Webb and Nelson). The black families in the real world who opened their homes in the way the Sledges do for Mack served as bridges, linking the aspirations of a new and revolutionary generation to the traditions of black ancestors. This was most true in the case of the Student Non-Violent Coordinating Committee members who went south to register blacks to vote. Unita Blackwell puts it eloquently: " 'We were all excited about these young people . . . because they was educated and they treated us so nice. All the educated folk we had known looked at us like we were fools and didn't know nothing, and these here talked to us like we was educating them' " (Giddings, 286). The respect that members of SNCC showed "uneducated" rural blacks translated into a revolutionary situation. Material distinctions were blurred by a commonality of struggle.

In the novel, the interaction between Mack and the Sledges provides a structure that serves to make Mack's destiny believable through the use of foreshadowing. Reba Sledge asks Mack about a woman he has been dating: " 'I guess I ain't got no right meddlin' in your private business. That's yo' business. But I just knowed a whole buncha colored men who done got messed up fooling with them Gitchee women.' " When Mack tells Mrs. Sledge that Michelle, the woman in question, is not "Gitchee" but Portuguese, she is relieved: " 'Well, I'm glad of that. Them's [Gitchee women] some wild heifers.' " She nevertheless concludes with a warning: " 'Watch yourself, you never know. There's so much happening these days' " (McCluskey, 19). Mrs. Sledge's maternal concern is paralleled by her husband. Mack has been unable to find a job playing his saxophone, and his money is running out. He tells Mr. Sledge of his plan to pick cranberries. Mr. Sledge tactfully deflates that idea by offering Mack the opportunity to work with him. " 'But I don't know anything about cabinets.' " Mr. Sledge is persistent and convincing, saying that " 'there ain't nothing to it. It's easy, like chunking rocks at a big barn' " (McCluskey, 12). Mack accepts the offer.

This parental concern does not suffocate Mack because it is obviated by the Sledges' healthy disrespect for precedents that are not in some way corroborated by their own experience. When Mack turns up at the Sledges' door, he is taken in as a matter of course: " 'Never turn a stranger from your door. He might be your best friend, you never know' " (McCluskey, 10). The curious looks of neighbors who have noticed that Mack drinks too much, does not work, blows his horn too loud, and looks too long at the young women's swaying hips do not concern the Sledges. Dupree Sledge notes that " 'people around here been acting damn funny since you come and I ain't never had no use for funny-acting folks' " (McCluskey, 11). The Sledges' personal compass is flexible because it adjusts to the force at hand. North and South, right and wrong are concepts that are internally derived.

Again, the Sledges' choice to stand outside the accepted bourgeois dogma concerning treatment of an outsider is similar to the perspective of many southern blacks who allowed the civil rights workers to stay in their homes. Of course, the danger that southern blacks who made this decision faced was more severe than the haughty, sideways glances of the Sledges' neighbors. The Sledges endured their negative neighbors with style, but those hospitable southern blacks may have suffered damage to their property or loss of life. "Those who sheltered the students could expect to be jailed, burned out, or subjected to the crudest violence" (Giddings, 284). The reaction, however, was not always docile or accepting: "When Whites shot at her home after she [Mrs. Silas McGhee] and her husband became involved with the movement, Mrs. McGhee called the sheriff and told him . . . she knew exactly who was out there shooting at her and that the sheriff should come and tell these here boys to go home, because they were going to be picking up bodies the next time that she called" (Giddings, 285). When a generation of young black men and women consciously seek out their preceding generations for guidance and help, the values of white society as well as existing social arrangements are challenged. This helps explain the fear and the resultant brutality that typified the white southern response to this part of the civil rights movement.

Although the Sledges are convinced of Mack's leadership qualities, he is, at best, a reluctant leader. Having tired of them hanging on to his every word, Mack explains that any leadership ability he has must be gounded in his music: "To say that I'm like a leader in any other way is to place a heavy weight on me. Just say I'm the one who woke folks up to themselves one dawn, blowing wild and beautiful changes" (McCluskey, 12–13). Of importance here is the division between the general leadership role that the Sledges thrust on Mack and the specific role he sees himself playing. The division becomes dramatic halfway through the novel when Mack reacts to the assassination of Martin Luther King, Jr. He becomes a revolutionary, but he quickly returns to the realization that his leadership is more creative than political.

Robert Moses, an important and charismatic leader during the early days of SNCC, was similar to Mack in that he too found his leadership to be more creative than political. Moses was unable to institutionalize his brilliance in a fashion that would allow others to take advantage of it. Instead, he counseled SNCC members to go where "the spirit say go and do what the spirit say do" (Roberts, 29). Clearly, this is not an attitude that makes for a smooth-running organization. Actually, Moses's dilemma, as well as Mack's, results because traditional organizational forms (certainly those that serve as models in various civics courses) are not capable of taking advantage of creative black politics. Put in the general context of literacy as it is being used here, the fictional and real-life characters who shape and are shaped by the events of the civil rights movement had to discover a tradition in African and Afro–American history that could develop their political creativity without distorting their personalities. Thus Robert Moses, Mack, and numerous other real-life and fictional characters are in the process of obtaining literacy. Without literacy, their political activity becomes a series of brilliant beginnings that end in slow and inevitable disappointments.

Before moving to New England, the Sledges lived in Lowndes County, Alabama, where another character comes in search of what Reba Sledge calls his "roots or something." That character is Andrew, also known as Antar. Although Andrew looks "all funny like we done just told him some bad news" when the Sledges ask him about his work, they are not put off: " 'You know and I know, some people made to do something while others ain't. God didn't tell the spider to make honey or the bee to spin webs and he didn't tell some men to study books who should been farming or singing along' " (McCluskey, 21). Wherever Andrew fits along the continuum is all right with the Sledges. In like manner, the funny looks of neighbors who question Mack's doleful presence in the Sledge household do not change the Sledges' feelings about him.

Antar is the son of a doctor and an implicit black bourgeois who goes south with a peculiar missionary zeal. The search for his roots is his initial thrust: " 'I guess that in the end I was down there like most everyone else. I was going to straighten out the South when I didn't

even know the first thing about it. And they didn't budge" (Mc-
Cluskey, 211–12). Here Antar sounds very much like Lynne
Rabinowitz, the wife of Truman Held in Walker's *Meridian*. Neither
character respects the traditions of the black community. Unlike
some of their bourgeois counterparts in the real world (Giddings,
282), Antar never relates to the lives of the people he hopes to change.
Indeed, Antar, the black idealist from "up north," his facile admission notwithstanding, is not, even in retrospect, capable of fully
understanding his relationship with the people he wants to change:
" 'All that time I was down there, you know, I never get them to
vote' " (McCluskey, 212). In an effort to explain these people, Mack
relates an incident that occurred while he lived with the Sledges in
New England. Dupree made and sold wine to black soldiers at a
nearby military base without being caught. Antar is unimpressed.
Although the caper may have netted Dupree personal satisfaction, it
did not alter the power relationships between blacks and whites.
Mack offers a more direct defense: " 'I think he [Dupree] was fighting
with everything he had. He was over seventy, man. It might have
been different with us, but he was an old man' " (McCluskey, 212).

Mack accepts the Sledges through an understanding which,
though critical, is enveloping. Dupree and Reba Sledge are a part of
his heritage, as are all older Afro-Americas: "They have their ways and
make their mistakes like us, but many of them are rocks to lean on"
(McCluskey, 212). This realization escapes Andrew, causing him to
regret that he never persuaded them to vote. Dupree's battlefield is
not the ballot box. His style is indirect, having more in common with
the double-talking oral tradition that obtained ends through circum-
locution than with the assertive tradition that obtained ends through
direct action.

Black voter registration, an important part of the civil rights
movement, cannot simply be an imperative. For it to have meaning it
must be rooted in the outlook of the people it is to benefit. No
amount of logic, even when documented by the most convincing
statistics, can transcend the fundamental necessity of accepting, then
working through, the outlook of older Afro–Americans. Mack, unlike Antar, knows this, but it takes the bulk of the novel for that
knowledge to become operative.

Mack's perspective on this issue has more in common with
SNCC leadership than does Antar's. SNCC leaders went to great

pains to make clear to their volunteers that they must respect the values and mores of blacks in southern communities whom they strove to help. To be sure, there was another side to SNCC and the civil rights movement, which sought to exploit the national attention being focused on black concerns, and this also gets attention in McCluskey's novel.

Ubangi, an affable though scheming character, is representative of this exploitive tradition. Structurally, he functions as an illuminating foil for Mack's character. Mack wants consistency built on a fusion of his music and relevant aspects of Afro-American history. Ubangi is all fluidity; his only defining characteristic is a desire to ride the crest of current trends. He has the hot air of the promoter, and it continually flows in a stream of assumed omniscience that often embarrasses Mack. He tells Mack to come to Boston: "I'm the one with the contacts up there and it's contacts that do it, Mack. I know them all up there. Anybody will tell you if you ain't got no contacts, you ain't got a pot to piss in" (McCluskey, 30). After several weeks in Boston, Mack is washing dishes and practicing his horn only occasionally. Ubangi is hustling and doing well. Although his contacts never materialize, Ubangi feels no impunity in chastising Mack for not practicing regularly: " 'You ain't touched your horn since we been up here. Shoot, these niggers up here is good too, Mack. I done heard them. . . . I'm going to see a contact in a few minutes. He might be able to do something for you. I don't want to get a job for you and you turn up shaky' " (McCluskey, 60). The two cease being roommates, and Mack, with Crackerjack's help, lands a club date at the Black Knight.

Meanwhile, Ubangi has hustled off to a "pimp's convention," which he vainly strove to get Mack to attend. Ubangi returns a new man. " 'You don't even look like yourself,' " Mack tells Ubangi. Ubangi wears "a white dashiki trimmed in rich red. A gold ankh dangles at his chest." Clearly impressed with himself, Ubangi asks Mack: " 'How would your militant friends like this?' " As usual, Ubangi has missed the mark: " 'Ubangi, they'd take you for an undercover man right off the bat. Your shoes. They're suede. They don't walk around wearing that kind of suede no more' " (McCluskey, 157). Ubangi shrugs his shoulders, a show of indifference.

Ubangi comfortably wears a dashiki and assumes that it connects him with a radical tradition in the black community. The symbolic dress associated with the black power movement is simply another guise for Ubangi to use to advance one of his various pursuits. Indeed, the idea of a pimp's convention is indicative of the way he thinks about the world. But like everything else he tries, Ubangi is not successful as a pimp. Ova Easy, the lone member of his "stable," not only turns out to be a transvestite, but provides the circumstances for Mack's and Ubangi's arrest. The episode temporarily deflates Ubangi's certainty, and he realizes that Mack is the only person on whom he can call for help. When a corrupt black policeman offers to let either Mack or Ubangi out if he is paid, Ubangi nods to Mack: " 'You go. You might do better than me gettin' some money' " (McCluskey, 175). Ubangi's tendency toward exploitation is too awkward to be taken seriously.

After being shipped to New Bedford for a trial on several charges and having those charges dropped—the star witness for the prosecution has an unexplained change of heart—Ubangi begins his final undertaking: "UBANGI'S UMOJA INSTITUTE FOR THE DARKER ARTS." What goes on in the institute is unclear. We know only that it is supposed to help black people. After a surreal trip through the building, Mack remarks to himself: "No doubt this scheme will be as shaky as all the others. Where does he stop with this?" Mack then notices that Ubangi "stands and looks sadly out the window"—an intimation of an end to Ubangi's constant posing.

The frenetic and spontaneous character of Ubangi's activity precludes action derived from historical understanding. Ironically, Ubangi Jones's name implies a historical consciousness—the African surname joined with the Euro-American last name. He is, after all, Afro-American, although McCluskey does not capitalize on the name in this fashion. In light of the character's actions, I think that his name symbolizes a search for literacy.

Ubangi's quest for literacy is symptomatic of the ahistorical and spontaneous character of some Afro-American political activity during the late sixties and early seventies. The shifting perspectives of individuals and organizations are representative: the Black Panthers went from a self-defense organization concerned with ending police brutality in the black community to a Marxist organization—a change some critics called radical integrationism (Baraka, *Raise,*– 105); SNCC threw whites out as their focus went from integrationism to nationalism; and H. Rap Brown, constantly hounded by policemen, went from revolutionary to mystic.

The changes in individual political choice and organizational direction did not rest on foundations as shaky as those that undergirded Ubangi's shifts, but they often exhibited the same facile concern with the need for discovering and using relevant precedents in African and Afro-American history to effect social change. Even SNCC, which was arguably the most progressive organization to emerge from this period, had to travel the same road as earlier blacks had traveled. The scenario goes as follows: naive Afro-American buys into the myth that equality in America is based on merit, pursues the myth, discovers America's endless duplicity in denying blacks rights, and is radicalized, choosing to organize his or her life along nationalist lines. This scenario, however, does not mean that the pursuit of literacy is fully conscious. It does mean that the myth of equality is dashed because it is only superfically obtainable. The desegregation of public accommodations and the legal end to economic disparities between blacks and whites did not signal an actual end to economic disparities between blacks and whites. Indeed, many sixties activists remarked in the seventies about the irony of achieving various legal goals and then not having the economic means to make the goals real (Marable, 31–33; Perry; Power). Such activists discovered that a new and more far-reaching form of social change was necessary to deal with these problems.

Within the swirl of events that motivate Ubangi and others like him, Mack, even though reticent, remains a rock. His stability is remarkable in light of Ubangi's constant changes. Like the Sledges in their relationship with Antar, Mack is able to accept Ubangi and stand by him. As Mrs. Sledge points out, " 'Some people made to do something while others ain't.' " Understanding that he does not know exactly what Ubangi's "something" is forces Mack away from a self-righteousness that would prevent helping a friend who repeatedly makes variations of the same mistakes.

The trip to New Bedford to lend moral support to Ubangi and the relationship with Novella Turner and consequently with Reverend C.E. Fuller further motivates Mack to fulfill his destiny, which is to blow his unity music to heal the various antagonisms within the black community. But it takes Wendell's accidental shooting to move

Mack to an awareness that mandates intermingling his various motivations.

Charges for which Ubangi is to be tried in New Bedford are
dropped, allowing Mack free time to visit friends at a nearby army
base. His friends, as well as black soldiers whom he does not know,
are different than he remembers them. He scrutinizes an old friend:
"It's a new G.A. I'm seeing. A tiny nationalist flag sticks out from a
beer can on the window sill. The fist at the gate [a black soldier gave
him the clinched–fist black power salute] . . . it falls in place. I pour
myself another drink and wonder if I've been the only one standing
still these past few months" (McCluskey, 195). Although reminded of
his inertia, Mack decides to go to a party with some of the black
soldiers. The host is the down-to-earth Captain Blackwell from
Quitman, Georgia. " 'It be like this mostly every Friday, Mack.
. . . We do it big around here' " (McCluskey, 196). After eating ribs
and drinking scotch, Mack finds a bed in Blackwell's house and
sleeps. In a dream he addresses an assembly of black people: "I speak
to them of freedom and an old gray-haired man stands and asks how,
and I tell them to join hands. He asks me how again and I whip out
maps of libraries, recording studios, homes of rich white folk, rifle
ranges, back rooms of juju men. He asks me when and before I can
answer he's upon me, shaking me wildly, his eyes crazed, his breath
hot on my face. Before I knew it, he's stolen my voice and is screaming
his own name. The crowd has followed him off, but not all have
deserted me. A few mold a statue around me" (McCluskey, 197). The
structural placement of the dream plays a role similar to that played
by the internal monologues in the beginning and the middle of the
novel: Mack reflects on his destiny in light of his present. The dream
reveals that Mack's revolution will grow from a historically based
spirituality. The spirituality is implied in joining hands and the
reference, once again, to juju men. History is implied by the reference to maps of libraries; one imagines the maps pointing the way to
obscure though important information on African and Afro-American history. Mack desires literacy, for only then can his destiny be
fully realized. Part of the literacy he must obtain requires fluency
with modern technology. In the dream, recording studios are as
important as libraries, for literacy can be advanced through any
number of channels. Mack's implicit feeling that people must be
socialized and politicized about their history before they can actually

commence changing their worlds is similar to the feelings of many cultural nationalists of this era. One of their favorite axioms was "free your mind and your ass will follow."

Mack, like many cultural nationalists of the era, felt that any Afro-American revolution would be protracted and that its most important aspect would not be random violence; rather, it would be Afro-Americans obtaining, developing, and maintaining a historical perspective. Such a perspective is tantamount to literacy, and it would make it impossible for blacks to participate in their own enslavement.

That a number of blacks follow the old man is indicative of the spontaneous quality of the historical period that provides the novel's context. On one level, the old man's preoccupation with "when" is ahistorical because it does not consider the crowd's level of political consciousness. Afro-American political struggle is replete with examples of failure and betrayal that result from attempts to short-circuit a historically based politicization or socialization of the people who are to struggle for change. The assumption is that shared pigmentation necessarily results in a given political outlook. Thus the politicization that occurs rests primarily on a recitation of shared pains and the obligatory condemnation of whites. Although this process was necessary and understandable, it did not focus on the deformity caused by that same oppression (Karenga). The deformities caused by centuries of racism—and by deformity I simply mean the emotional, physical, and spiritual problems that result from a constrained and circumscribed existence—surely contributed to the energetic and sometimes misguided attempts at social change that went on during the sixties (Sellers, Marable). Put another way, the opportunities for self-determination provided by the black power movement were used by some Afro-Americans to justify intensely personal concerns.

An easy example is that some black men who were activists used the turn to Africa for cultural precedents as a basis to continue questionable activity. Amiri Baraka writes:

> Some of us were influenced by the Yorubas because we could understand a connection we had with Africa and wanted to celebrate it. We liked the African garb that Serj [Baba Oserjaman, a cultural nationalist] and his people wore. The lovely long dresses, the bubbas and lappas and gales of the women. After so much exposure to white women, the graceful dress of the

sisters in their African look, with their natural hair, turned us on. Plus Oserjaman and the rest talked about and practiced polygamy, and certainly for some of us who were used to ripping and roaring out of one bed and into another, this "ancient custom of our people" provided a perfect outlet for male chauvinism, now disguised as "an ancient custom of our people." (Baraka, *Autobiography*, 215–16)

So, with the blessings of the "ancestors," some of the most reactionary elements in the black community could cloak their actual desires. In many cases, these desires clearly preceded any political concern.

Ubangi, the old man, and the other specters that people Mack's dreams are clearly examples of the above discussion. But Mack is steadfast, even though he is confused as to where and how he will fulfill his destiny. Mack's feeling that "a man can usually find out where he's at and where he's going by the type of woman he is messing with" (McCluskey, 14) suggests that his destiny will not be fulfilled until he is completed, in balance. His concern is in keeping with much of the rhetoric of the sixties that described ideal relationships between black men and women. Numerous poems, plays, and essays were written which extolled the necessity of black women and men uniting on new and highly political planes (Jones and Neal). Interestingly, in the real world, black women sought such relationships much more than did men. So Mack is a bit rare in his desire to develop a monogamous relationship that will help him develop his potential. Early in the novel he bemoans his plight:

"I cried lord have mercy
Lord have mercy on me
I'm trying to find my baby
Won't somebody send her home to me." (McCluskey, 9)

In New England, without a woman to weld his various impulses together, he writes the following verse:

"I keep drifting and drifting like a ship out
to sea
I keep drifting and drifting like a ship out
to sea
I ain't got nobody in this world to care for
me." (McCluskey, 24)

More than halfway through the novel we meet Novella Turner; she is divorced and has a daughter. She is able to weld the pieces of

Mack's personality together because of her spirituality and because of what she learns as one of three blacks who integrate an all-white school in Charlotte, North Carolina. Women with whom Mack has previously associated lack both of these attributes. They are merely beautiful baubles, casually bouncing from one set of imperatives to another.

Mack and Novella are more visionary than activist because of their spiritual outlook. Mack tells us that they "talked about her music and my music and how they flowed from one spirit, one need" (McCluskey, 230). Their visionary politics allows them to take the long view toward social change. In some ways their view is similar to that of early civil rights activists. The centrality of spirituality in their struggle made it possible for them to withstand the unbelievable brutality they encountered in their various marches and demonstrations. Their spirituality made it possible for them to see beyond the moment and to envision a time when racism was not the defining force in black/white relations. For such activists, in fiction and in the real world, spirituality provides a vision that allows the defeat of a seemingly unbeatable foe.

Although Mack intuitively knows that Novella is capable of helping him realize his destiny, it is hard for him to let go of his insecurities. Novella, however, is not content to glimpse Mack: " 'Come on now, you give out those little pieces of yourself like it's killing you, like I'm going to run something on you. . . . But Mack, I can't play slick. When the feeling is there, it's there and I can't do a damn thing about it except to give in to it' " (McCluskey, 230). Novella's emotional giving and the gentle demand that it be reciprocated is exactly what Mack has thirsted for, and her membership at Crumbly Rock Baptist Church provides a gateway to an institutional setting for Mack to blow his music. Reverend Fuller is contemplating retirement and is unsatisfied with the coterie of possible replacements who wait in the wings. With the following explanations, he offers Mack Crumbly Rock Baptist Church: " 'Lots of folks want to see the church stay the way it was a long time ago. Now, don't get me wrong. Ain't nothing wrong with the old times except they be old times. They ain't new times. Crumbly Rock Baptist needs a modern man, a man who can handle the young ones when their blood gets warm and they want to be out in the street whooping and hollering with their friends, and a man who can handle the old ones who are strong as oak and set in their ways' " (McCluskey, 207–8). Reverend Fuller's vision is simply another expression of Mack's unity music. The entire community is to be brought together, with each generation respecting and learning from the other. Under this equation, change flows from the bottom up as well as from the top down. The world envisioned is an egalitarian one. Revolutionary imperatives, political or spiritual, cannot be imposed on the community. As was the case with the SNCC workers who sought to help blacks in the South, solutions to problems must come through or be merged with belief systems that exist in the community. To do less is to disrespect the people one intends to help.

This insight is slow to penetrate Antar's hard head. When he hears of Mack's plan to invite representatives from all segments of the black community to Crumbly Rock Baptist Church, Antar contorts his face and speaks " 'Mix the righteous with unrighteous, Mack?' " This is exactly what Mack proposes. The nationalists, the integrationists, and members of fringe groups of the Left and Right are all welcome at Crumbly Rock. Mack feels that to do otherwise is to heighten the chances of antagonistic whites pitting one group against another, which would be reminiscent of the racial betrayal that prompted the slave trade. Mack feels that his unity music can transcend the various rituals of different political groups that hinder operational unity.

The events that spur Mack to attempt to unify various segments of the black political community have parallels in the real world. The first National Black Political Convention held in Gary, Indiana, in 1972, as well as the 1974 convention held in Little Rock, Arkansas, are the best examples of a national attempt to do what Mack set out to do. The convention in Gary strove for "unity without uniformity." As the Sledges might say, "everyone ain't meant to do the same thing." The convention was like a national Crumbly Rock Baptist Church. Both institutions provide a context for black creativity. Mack's unity music cannot be played at Carnegie Hall; nor is it possible for the Democratic or Republican party to devise an agenda that advances the goals of the masses of black people. Although the convention movement did not accomplish its goals, the attempt suggested possibilities beyond those posed by established political parties.

It is also significant that McCluskey chooses music as a basis for black unity. Black music served that function at various points during the civil rights movement. Paula Giddings writes about the efforts of the National Association for the Advancement of Colored People, the Southern Christian Leadership Conference, and SNCC to organize black residents of Albany, Georgia: "It would take a special effort to keep the disparate pieces of the Albany Movement together, and SNCC discovered a vital key to that unity. That key, which would be used in subsequent SNCC actions, was music. It was song, the heart of Black Cultural expression, that provided the cohesive force to hold the different groups together. Albany became known as the 'singing movement.' It was the rich, darkly timbered voice of Bernice Reagon, an Albany State student who joined SNCC, that evoked the resonances of centuries-old memories" (Giddings, 283). Reagon's singing simply and profoundly connected blacks to their history. Although individuals still faced the struggle of discovering themselves in the context of history, music at least gave them definitive and irreducible foundation from which their quests might proceed. Reagon continues to mix music and politics as a leader of the singing group Sweet Honey in the Rock.

For Wendell, the foundation is provided by the crush of events. He is mistaken for a nationalist leader, and his near fatal shooting has left him a changed man: " 'I don't know what I'll be after I get out, but I'll be a different man. Before, I thought I could be the great actor, now I'm convinced I have no choice but to become one. In a hurry' " (McCluskey, 240). Mack's decision to accept Reverend Fuller's offer can be viewed in this light. Wendell's situation also provides the occasion for Novella to reflect on her participation as a child in the desegregation of a white school:

> There were fifty others in the town like us who might have come, but it came down to the three of us, our fathers really, because they did the deciding. They soaked up that mess for all the ones who didn't come that year—for our brothers and sisters all those who would come ten, twenty years from then. And we had to believe in that, past, present and future, but most of all in ourselves. We were finding something to fight with—we had sense enough to know we were in a fight then and the best part of ourselves would remain in the fight. What you choose to fight with becomes the biggest part of you. (McCluskey, 241)

For all these characters to fight with the biggest part of themselves, they must first accept themselves. There is nothing in one's personal or racial past to be ashamed of; through love, or the "spirit touch" as

Mack would say, it can all be appropriated. Reverend Fuller preaches his farewell sermon, and Mack then blows his unity music. His last lines—"In the beginning there's the spirit touch"—return us to the novel's prologue, for he has returned to that moment of the "first native betrayal" and corrected it with healing love.

Interwoven in Mack's development are political considerations that nudge him toward his destiny. Unlike characters in the novels previously discussed, he is more reticent than naive about his function in the political world. Like other characters, external demands draw him out: Malcolm X's assassination causes him to seek an environment sympathetic to his music and the assassination of Martin Luther King, Jr., causes him to rethink his life. Though these events cause reflection, they do not result in an abdication of personal history. He cannot will himself to become someone else's version of a revolutionary. In this sense, Mack has no problems. He has to accept his destiny. The love he advocates is the external message suggested to various black political and religious leaders who would squeeze the whole of the Afro-American experience into a narrow vision. Black reality is finally too immense to be captured under the thin magic of slogans.

References

Aptheker, Herbert. *American Negro Slave Revolts.* New York: International Publishers, 1943.

Baraka, Amiri. *The Autobiography of Leroi Jones.* New York: Freundlich Books, 1984.

———. *Raise Race Rays Raze.* New York: Random House, 1971.

Black Scholar. May–June, 1979.

Cruse, Harold. "The Black Political Convention." *Black World,* October 1974, pp. 10–17.

Daniels, Ron. "The National Black Political Assembly: Building Independent Black Politics in the 1980s." *Black Scholar,* March–April 1978, pp. 11–15.

Giddings, Paula. *When and Where I Enter . . . . : The Impact of Black Women on Race and Sex in America.* New York: Morrow, 1984.

Karenga, Ron. "A Strategy for Struggle." *Black Scholar,* November 1973, pp. 8–21.

Jones, Leroi, and Larry Neal, eds. *Black Fire: An Anthology of Afro–American Writing.* New York: Morrow, 1968.

Long, Richard. "The Symbolization of Black Consciousness: Anatomy of a Failure." CAAS Occasional Paper 12. Atlanta: *Center for African and African–American Studies,* Atlanta University, n.d.

McCluskey, John. *Look What They Done to My Song.* New York: Random House, 1974.

Marable, Manning. *How Capitalism Underdeveloped Black America.* Boston: South End Press, 1983.

Napier, George. *Blacker Than Thou.* Berkeley: Eerdman, 1973.

Perry, T. D. "Black Power Five Years Later." *Negro History Bulletin,* November 1971, pp. 148–49.

Power, J. "Whither the Black Power Movement." *Current,* November 1971, pp. 21–24.

Roberts, Gene. "The History of Snick: From 'Freedom High' to 'Black Power.' " *New York Times Magazine,* 25 September 1966, pp. 27–29, 19–20, 122, 124, 126, 128.

Sellers, Cleve. *River of No Return.* New York: Morrow, 1973.

Webb, Sheyann, and Rachel West Nelson. *Selma, Lord Selma.* University, Ala.: University of Alabama Press, 1980.

8

The Cotillion
as Symbol and Reality

The social backdrop of *The Cotillion or One Good Bull Is Half the Herd* is that part of the black power movement which advocated name changes, African attire, and other outward expressions of black consciousness as methods for Afro-Americans to exercise self-determination. Within this context, the novel explores the contradiction between appearance and reality by illustrating the interaction of Afro-American and Euro-American symbols. We see different members of the black community respond to the same set of symbols in glaringly different ways. As one might expect, the cotillion is the central symbol. In its purest state, the cotillion is presented as European, derived from eighteenth-century France. Yet, like so many European cultural expressions, once Afro-Americans "get hold" of them, their texture and flavor are dramatically altered. So, in one sense, the characters are in conflict as to how "black" a cotillion can be. More specifically, one group of characters is determined to have the black cotillion be as European as possible, whereas another group questions the extent to which the form itself (the cotillion) can be made to serve black needs.

Thus the major conflicts in the novel result from characters trying to balance the symbolic demands made by the black power movement with the demands made by their own personal histories. Those who run from any mention of Africa must shed an unattractive bourgeois veneer which is cracked and crumbling with age and, in a sense, be born again. Those who champion "Mother Africa" must move from their plateaus of symbolic correctness and merge with that which is good about black people regardless of their symbolic wrappings. They are faced with the task of obtaining freedom and literacy in an environment in which meanings associated with symbols constantly shift. For the major characters—Lumumba, Yoruba, and Lady Daphne—to obtain freedom and literacy, each must understand the meanings of symbols in the context of his or her personal history and then apply those symbols; only then does a dashiki, a "natural," or a buba leave the plane of "hip" or radical fashion and become a part of their lives. The characters must learn that the consciousness associated with these styles precedes and goes beyond actually wearing them; it is a question of attitude. The older members of the black middle class portrayed in the novel do not obtain literacy because they do not reflect on the meanings associated with Euro-American symbols that animate their lives. As a consequence, their social affairs are supremely vacuous rituals which serve to separate them from the masses of black people.

All the characters in the novel are affected by the symbolic dimensions of political struggle and must, as a consequence, learn to distinguish between appearance and reality. Functionally, their struggle makes them hard to know and in some cases it makes them purely exploitive. Yoruba Lovejoy's first affair is with Jaja Okwu—born Bobby Jack Sampson. Jaja is determined to politicize Yoruba. The extraneous goes first: " 'Drop out of school. . . . It ain't relevant to the Black experience. . . . I got your education, Sister Yoruba. You just let this proud black man take care of business.' " His educational alternative is direct, even if patchwork: " 'Read Fanon and Mao and all them other people' " (Killens, 81) is what he tells his pupil.

Actually Jaja's advice is in keeping with some of the rhetoric of the black power movement concerning the necessity for a people involved in a struggle for self-determination to educate their own children (Madthubuti). The most constructive side of this advice resulted in the creation of African free schools and a plethora of black research organizations. The less constructive side resulted in random reductionisms which questioned the relevancy of all fields of knowledge that did not have an immediate practical dimension. I recall, for example, a speech that Amiri Baraka made at Indiana University in 1972 in which he admonished black students to learn to do something concrete. He asked, "Can you build a radio station? Can you construct a house?" The questions were posed after he had under-valued humanistic study as largely irrelevant to the coming revolu-tion; indeed, the study of English and history were seen as part of an elaborate socialization mechanism tied to maintaining "white power."

The way Baraka chose to deal with the relationship of education to Afro-American self-determination had the effect of undervaluing the various methods of coping with and altering situations which Afro-Americans had developed over time. In the broadest sense, the Afro-American propensity for improvisation is a combination of the theoretical (often derived from humanistic study) and the practical. Improvisation thus shatters the either/or dichotomy that inspired Baraka's speech, replacing it with a flexible both/and dichotomy. Perhaps a more fruitful approach would have accented that which could be "Afro-Americanized" in humanistic study and thereby made to serve the goals of Afro-American self-determination. Indeed, one can read Baraka's *The System of Dante's Hell, The Dead Lecturer,* and several of his plays ("Madheart, a Black Morality Play" comes imme-diately to mind) as reinventions or improvisations upon existing forms. To be sure, all of this is hindsight, for at the time I was en-ergetically among those students who applauded what seemed like the purest wisdom.

For Jaja Okwu, questions of self-determination are not very complex. Like some of the characters in McCluskey's novel and some of the lesser individuals in the real world, he used the racial quest for self-determination to advance very sorry personal needs. Having tired of "the torrid love scenes that always come up short of the actual act of intimacy," Jaja makes his pupil's role clear: " 'If you going to be my baby, sister, you going to have to get out there on the block and sell it, while I organize for the revolution' " (Killens, 81).

Less exploitive but equally at variance with their appearance are "a group of rip-snorting militants [who] stood in a corner of the basement rec-room, off to themselves, burning incense to the Gods of Pot." The scene reminds one of the militants, Casey Bingbop, of another good time: ' "One night we had a grass party at my crib in Boston, we threw up such a smokescreen my neighbor thought the house was on fire' " (Killens, 213). The neighbor turns in a fire alarm and " 'The whole damn motherfucking Boston Fire Department came down on us. Broke into my pad and started chopping every-thing.' " Not one to allow injustice to go uncorrected, Casey pursued the matter: " 'Dig. We brought charges against the fire department for violation of our civil rights. We accused them of attacking us because we were Black militants. Fifth amendment, due process, and all that motherfucking shit' " (Killens, 213–14). Jaja and Casey are infinitely phonier than they first appear, using the goals of the black power movement for narrow personal ends.

By mixing realistic and satiric modes of expression, Killens presents the black middle class as caught in a bizarre universe of Euro-American symbols. Their slick refinement is riddled by an ignorance that is remarkable in its multiple and consistent expression. In response to a question about her musical taste, Mrs. Robinson, a member of the middle class, says:

> [Mrs. Robinson] "Oi don't like jazz, blues, spearchels and that kind of common averyday music. Oi prefer the clausics. Oi like Chopping."
> [Mrs. Jefferson] "I'm hip. Everybody like chopping. You have to eat to live, but I thought we were discussing music."
> [Mrs. Robinson] "Chopping. . . . He's a great European musician. He lives in Paris."
> [Mrs. Brap-bap] "She means Chopin," she explained to Mrs. Jefferson. Then to Mrs. Robinson she said, "Honey, you can't even pronounce him, let alone appreciate him." (Killens, 138–39)

Mrs. Brasswork, who flunked out of three law schools, also assumes poses that suggest more than is actually there. When her daughter continuously fawns over Yoruba, Mrs. Brasswork reprimands: " 'Will you cease and discontinue? . . . You're displaying prima facie evi-dence of bad upbringing and ill manners' " (Killens, 208). Mrs. Brasswork's command of legalese is severely tested when cotillion participants decide to wear Afros. While trying to stop the Afroed debutantes from going on stage, she snags her hoop skirt and is distressed: " 'Ipso facto! Certiori! Sine qua non! Prima Facie! Shit! Damn! Hell! Motherfucker! Fifth Amendment!' " (Killens, 283). The torn hoop skirt and black debutantes who choose to wear their hair in Afros are too much for her: " 'Quid pro quo! Res ajudica! Kiss my ass! With all deliberate speed!' " Mrs. Robinson's and Mrs. Brass-work's attempts to display cultural elegance and worldliness are humorously interpenetrated by rowdy ignorance.

The middle-class characters are relatively flat, predictable types who serve to illustrate the most limiting and reactionary aspects of the black community.

The more interesting characters tend to resemble chameleons. Trying to impress Yoruba's mother, Lumumba (born Ernest Walter Billings) has his natural trimmed to a respectable length and sheds his dashiki for a three-piece suit. He is on his best behavior: " 'Well, well, I had almost forgotten what an elegant lady your mother was, Yoruba.' " Miss Daphne, Yoruba's mother, is caustic though impressed: " 'Well, I must say, Ernest, you have certainly changed, and, from appearance, it has all been for the better' " (Killens, 183). Yoruba is not impressed by Lumumba's metamorphosis, for she sees it as an abdication of his African ancestry: "Why couldn't she understand that he'd done it all as a joke, a snow job on her mother? Why didn't she understand that he'd done it all for her, his Yoruba? The bush, the beard, the African garb. He was not a member of an organization that wore them as a uniform. He had not betrayed the cause. The cause was not hair or beard or dashiki. And after all, he was the same person afterward" (Killens, 192). The symbolization of Afro-American attempts at self-definition further complicates the contradiction between appearance and reality. Can one, after all, assign consistent meaning to symbols? Yoruba certainly has problems in answering this question; for her the meaning of the cotillion alters. She first resists it, then embraces it to satisfy her mother; she later attempts to redefine it in a black image. After having redefined it, she contemplates fleeing it, feeling that participation would be wrong. Lumumba understands this last panic. " 'It's not easy to make a break with the present past,' " he tells Yoruba as he kisses away her tears. For Yoruba and Lumumba, changes in symbolic appearance do not signal changes in outlook. Such changes, like the adaptive coloration of the chameleon, are tactical.

By shifting the point of view between first, second, and third person, Killens manages to make the contradiction between appearance and reality very clear. Just when we are able to gauge the novel's point of view it shifts. The foreword is in the voice of the central character, Ben Ali Lumumba. He lets us know that the novel's structure, like the structured reality of black people, is an improvisation, a blending of different voices to create a functioning whole.

Lumumba tells us that the novel will be a "Black, black comedy" meant to signify. "I [mean] to let it all hang out" (Killens, 13).

Although the black middle class as portrayed in the novel suffers most from this signifying, no segment of the black community—conservative, militant, or liberal—is spared. Signifying requires free movement and an associational expression that does not limit itself to clear categories based on generally accepted rules of discourse. Lumumba informs us: "Like I went to one of them downtown white workshops for a couple of months and got all screwed up with angles of narration, points of view, objectivity, universality, composition, author-intrusion, sentence structure, syntax, first person, second person. I got so screwed up I couldn't unwind myself for days. I said to hell with all that. I'm the first, second and third person my own damn self. And I will intrude, protrude, obtrude or exclude my point of view any time it suits my disposition" (Killens, 12). Having made explicit the contours of his poetic license, Lumumba indicates that they will be molded by "Black idiom, Black nuances, Black style. Black truths, Black exaggerations." The musical referent for the amalgamation is improvisational jazz—a fusion of several black musical traditions. The linguistic referent, according to Lumumba, is "Afro-Americanese, Black rhythm, baby." Improvisation informed by recurring rhythms dictated by a desire to "speak the truth" describes the method of Lumumba's signifying. This approach creates a point of view that defines itself in motion. *The Cotillion* thus appears as a novel always reaching toward literacy.

The fluidity of "Afro-Americanese" makes the shifts in point of view inconsequential because it captures what is linguistically, philosophically, and politically black. Who is telling the story is less important than how the story is told. The reader must take Lumumba's claim—"I'm the first, second and third person"—seriously. Signifying holds the improvisation together.

There are thirteen chapters, the first seven of which have straightforward titles: "Yoruba," "Matthew" (Yoruba's father), "Daphne," "Lumumba," and so forth. Later chapter titles reflect the unleashing of the signifying in which Killens engages. The absurdity of the situations depicted is suggested by such titles as "Eenie Meenie," "The Really Real Thing," "To Wig or Not to Wig," and "Ye Olde Plantation." The first fourth of the novel provides personal histories of Yoruba, Daphne, Matthew, and Lumumba, the major characters, in a way that makes clear why they relate to the cotillion as they do. Matthew is a nationalist who "had marched behind every Black man who ever raised his voice in Harlem, including Garvey, Powell, Ben Davis, Paul Robeson, and very naturally, Brother Malcolm" (Killens, 48). His wife is Lady Daphne, a West Indian mulatto, who "was the kind of proud Caribbean beauty who loftily cherished her British heritage. The only songs that really made her heart leap wildly and warmly wet her eyes were 'God Save the Queen' and 'Rule Britannia' " (Killens, 59). Yoruba is proud of her blackness, more her father's daughter than her mother's. Lumumba is on the end of the political spectrum opposite Lady Daphne.

Of the main characters, it is Lady Daphne who nakedly aligns herself with the Femme Fatales, the black middle-class organization that works to spread "culture." The changes that Lady Daphne, Lumumba, and Yoruba experience in their shifting feelings about the relationship to the cotillion and, in a general sense, all white symbols, suggests the possibilities and limitations of black political activity that focuses on racial definition through the creation, definition, and redefinition of symbols.

Killens's decision to have the character with the most reactionary politics, Lady Daphne, portrayed as a tragic mulatto is significant because of the role that complexion played in superficially defining people's politics during the black power movement. In many instances, particularly at black power conferences and various black student union meetings, white characteristics such as long, straight hair and light skin tone signaled reactionary or integrationist politics. In tying into this aspect of the black power movement, Killens does not limit himself to the possibilities suggested by the events that occurred during this period. Instead, in his treatment of Lady Daphne he suggests a way out of assigning meaning based solely on appearances. Lady Daphne can be and is ultimately helped to move beyond the notions she has about what is possible in black life. Significantly, this occurs because her family and friends love and care for her. Through them, she begins the process of achieving literacy.

Lady Daphne is best understood within the context of her mixed ancestry. Angus Braithwaite, her father, "a big important white man," is "rather generous to his thirty to forty-five colored children." Her mother, much to Lady Daphne's chagrin, finds herself out of favor because she "didn't understand the limitations of a concubine's prerogatives. In a word, she was a sassy Black woman, gave ol masser word for word" (Killens, 47). Despite being the offspring of a dispossessed concubine, Lady Daphne still sees herself as a Braithwaite, a member of the "first family of Barbados." Though not white, she is certainly not black; her white features are not dominant, but her white attitude is. Lady Daphne is a mulatto aristocrat who, on arriving in America, maintains a self-concept infinitely superior to what objective circumstances might suggest. Such feelings of superiority are not very useful when they make it impossible for characters or individuals in the world to adjust to or to change their material circumstances. In America, Lady Daphne finds work as a hotel maid: "She told the other girls with whom she worked, when they complained of the clientele laying hands on them as if they were faith healers, 'It's all the way you carry yourself, my dears. They ain't dare put their hands on me. They know character when they see it' " (Killens, 57). The assumption that appearances are absolute—"They know character when they see it"—is false. Lady Daphne tenders her resignation after the hotel manager refuses to evict an aggressive male occupant who chased her around his bed.

Although she lacks a material base and the education to give her aristocratic attitude objective expression, Lady Daphne holds tight to that attitude. The variance between the way she sees herself and what she is capable of doing creates a chasm of nonreality. Into that chasm are poured all the marvelous symbols associated with Euro-American grace and beauty. The cotillion is of course the primary symbol in this respect. She contemplates a wondrous future for her daughter, as she discusses the upcoming cotillion: " 'You are indeed a lucky one . . . and of all the scrumptious places, it will be downtown at the Waldorf, where few white folks get a chance to go and decidedly no niggers at all. . . . The grand magnificent Cotillion. It's everything I've worked for dearie. The opportunity of a lifetime. My own daughter is going to be a debutante' " (Killens, 34). The West Indian mulatto, having only seen blacks and mulattoes grovel at the feet of whites in Barbados, claims and champions her white ancestry. Though that choice has not found expression in her life, it will flourish in her daughter's life.

Because her attempts to infuse Yoruba with a passion for "society" seldom evoke the desired response, Lady Daphne adapts tactics that revise her personal history. Though having obvious practical utility, the tactics also soothe psychological needs that are pastoral in outlook. Lady Daphne complains bitterly: " 'I turned my back on my father's house, on all his wealth and riches, gave up everything for this family here. Gave up the easy life for a life of strife and struggle. And all I have to show for it is a good heart done gone bad and broken, so many times, so many times! And my own baby do not love me' " (Killens, 70). She conveniently forgets that the "turning" was not hers to do; her mother's "sassiness" took care of that. The martyrlike tone of her outburst suggests a frame of mind that is both paranoid and manipulative. She sometimes feels absolutely outside the world that Matt and Yoruba fashion through their smiles and warm chuckles. Her exclusion is a function of her pretentiousness. Nevertheless, her family loves her, and she manipulates their love through paranoid outbursts.

Given Lady Daphne's cultural proclivities, why she marries Matt is initially puzzling. He is dark complected, nationalistic, and decidedly folksy. Lady Daphne can be magnanimous: " 'I don't hold your father's color against him,' " she tells Yoruba. She does eventually change enough to confront her past openly in the context of her present. She explains to Yoruba about having married Matt: " 'Because every white man I met in this country had no respect for me. And I swear a long time ago, I kissed the Good Book, that I ain't never be the white man's whore. . . . Or his concubine like my mother was. . . . And your father, he respected me. Respected me too much sometimes. And I married him, because he was Black and respected me. And I thought that he was beneath me and would bow down to me, his fair queen from Barbados. . . . But through the years, I learned to love and respect him' " (Killens, 246). Her marriage is an attempt to assure a life of self-respect, and it suggests an elemental level of black consciousness—one might say that it exists in spite of her character—that puts limits on self-debasement. Although Lady Daphne can chastise her mother for being sassy and not knowing her place, she cannot or will not assume the place her mother occupied.

Yoruba has little interest in becoming a "lady" because she is after a "new world": "In Yoruba's new world, Black was the 'in thing' and the 'end thing.' Alpha and Omega, or words in Swahili to that effect. . . . Yoruba had been to Black happenings where the brothers and sisters of the darkest complexion did violent putdowns of those unfortunates of the lighter hues, all in the spirit of black unity. She had even caught herself at evil moments, bugging her mother because her mother's color had suddenly become unstylish. . . . 'You ought to get out in the sun more often mother. You don't want to be mistaken for a honkie' " (Killens, 88–89). Yoruba is involved in the process of defining beauty based on an Afro-American aesthetic. White is evil and black is good: light-skinned blacks are closest to evil and dark-skinned blacks are closest to good. Radical racial redefinition also disallows blind acceptance of European artifacts: a cotillion, after all, fails to speak to Yoruba's reality. It is, at best, an imitation of an aristocratic ritual, the history of which has little to do with people of African descent. Yoruba wants a new world in which an Afro-American aesthetic will be the primary basis for creating meaningful symbols. Yoruba finds, however, that racial redefinition does not supersede her love for her mother. Her remark about her mother's complexion—which is a function of her political involvement—and then her eventual backing away from it indicate that Yoruba's new black politics are not entirely her own.

An assertiveness followed closely by either snarled denials or muted apologies was a striking aspect of the black power movement's cultural nationalist dimension. Such people as Ron Karenga, Amiri Baraka, and, to a lesser extent, Haki Madthubuti, were unequaled in their ability to "talk bad" about black people who were not living up to their notions of blackness. This tendency is similar to Yoruba's actions in that these individuals and others like them sought to assign consistent meanings to symbols and appearances. Further, such individuals made political leaps of consciousness in assigning meaning in the context of their own experience. Baraka, in particular, with his Bohemian and interracial history, should, I would think, be most understanding. He treats his past nonchalantly and focuses on the pressing and immediate present. As Meridian tells Truman Held in Walker's novel, one cannot be involved in history and pretend that it never happened. To some extent, the sad march back to respectability that some black power advocates now make is a dramatic illustration of Yoruba's dilemma. That dilemma involves the personal problems that occur when the quest for literacy is advanced through someone else's point of view. Yoruba and those like her in the world were faced with the task of using their personal histories as a framework to

organize the various symbolic demands of the black power movement. When personal history does not work in this fashion, the
resulting politics are unpredictable and often contradictory.

A similar ambiguity exists with Lumumba. He reads his "black
art" poetry at an uptown cafe:

> It's here my brothers, here, here, here!
> Not in Paris or in Rome.
> Not in Denmark or in Sweden
> The fight is right back here at home,
> But they all tripped off to Europe,
> Where things were nice and fine.
> You could get your fill of pussy,
> But no jobs were for your kind
> If you can make it just on pussy,
> Run to Europe fast.
> But if you can't live on straight-haired cunt alone,
> that's gone be your fat Black ass.
> (Killens, 74)

Yoruba is impressed. His reading complete, Lumumba bows to a
wildly appreciative audience and decides to join Yoruba. He asks if a
seat at Yoruba's table is taken: "'Do you mind if I sit here a moment?'
It was a voice unlike the one he'd read his poetry with. All his
blackness seemed to have vanished in the darkness of the dark." She
allows him to sit but is thoroughly disappointed. Once seated, "He
smiled and motioned importantly to the waiter, '*Garcon, s'il vous
plaît*—, and turned to her again. 'Would you have something a little
more potent with me, Miss-Miss-Miss?' " (Killens, 77). Yoruba
wants only Coke and tells Lumumba she will pay for it. Unruffled, he
asks the waiter to " 'bring the lady another Coke, *s'il vous plaît*, and
bring me a bit of sherry of your oldest vintage?' " (Killens, 78).

This show of grace and style contradicts the poetry. If "it" is "not
in Paris," as he informs the audience, then why transport the French?
Why use it in a situation and a context that is self-consciously
attempting to be black? Like Truman Held in *Meridian*, Lumumba
adopts a European posture to impress. He substitutes *si'l vous plaît* for
Held's *Je m'appele*, but to more revealing ends: Lumumba's initial
appearance is that of a conscious Afro-American struggling to wake
his brothers and sisters from a heavy sleep induced by stultifying
Euro-American symbols. To treat his slumbering "sister" to French is

to risk deepening that sleep. Fortunately for both of them, Yoruba is not impressed by this show and ultimately forces Lumumba to end his pretensions.

Again, with Lumumba Killens shows us another dimension of the black power movement. Baraka and others labeled the black arts movement the spiritual sister of the black power movement. The drama and poetry associated with this movement were very much like that Lumumba read. Black art relied on the street for imagery and rhythms and a straightforwardness that made many whites and some blacks uncomfortable. Beyond the stylistic similarities between the "fictional" poetry in the novel and that produced by Don L. Lee (Haki Madthubuti), Sonia Sanchez, and other participants in the black arts movement is a challenge to live the lifestyle and values that animate the poetry. Although Lumumba and black poets in the real world were able to identify some of the stifling aspects of symbols and images associated with Euro-American culture, they were not always able to get beyond those symbols and images. It was easier to point out what needed changing than actually to change one's own personality. In a sense, this is the challenge of all people who attempt to change society: they must first and consistently change themselves.

Here I am being charitable. Some people caught in the contradiction between racial advocacy and personal practice worked only to prevent those they ostensibly sought to help from seeing that chasm. I have already discussed how some people used the national attention to black concerns as a cloaking device to work out their own intensely personal problems that preceded the movement. None of this is meant to undercut the role racism plays in deforming Afro-Americans, but it is meant to assert that political movements are not the best place for people to work out personal problems. Political activism, be it by someone in the world or by a fictional charcter, has to be internalized in a fashion that is congruent with the strengths and weaknesses of the activists. This is the highest form of literacy.

Certainly, Lumumba has not internalized the meanings and consequences associated with the symbolic vessel that carries his poetry. Yoruba reacts as follows to his reading: "Who was this wailing cat? Delivering his poetic thing 'Roi-Jones-Dante-Graham-Sheep-Askia-Muhammed Toure fashion, shoulders hunched forward into the storm, head dancing side to side, Afro-life-style, body rocking with the rhythm of a down home Baptist preacher" (Killens, 75).

Lumumba is a confluence of images from the black experience, and as such he carried meaning beyond himself—at least for Yoruba. By tapping the tradition of the signifier who speaks directly, rhythmically, and with the correctness of a Baptist preacher, Lumumba has taken on responsibilities that demand logical consistency. One cannot rationally urge the masses to leave Europe—surely an aesthetic imperative that interpenetrates all aspects of style—and then needlessly fall into linguistic and stylistic imitations of that same Europe.

Maintaining logical consistency when extending the consequences of adhering to a set of African or Afro-American symbols vexed many black power advocates. Like Lumumba, they often made aesthetic choices that contradicted the logical extensions of their rhetoric. The inclusive assertion that "Black Is Beautiful" was often contradicted by the black man's personal choice for romance or sex. For some, seducing the white woman became a political act that functioned to dash the symbolic claim that "Black Is Beautiful." The number of black men who took this action is less important than the apparent reason: a simple failure to deal with the consequences of one's advocacy in a personal fashion, the failure to interpenetrate political activism with personal history. Thus, although such men appeared to be at the zenith of political and historical understanding, they were actually illiterates. Lumumba is fortunate to have Yoruba set him straight.

Lumumba is a confident talker. He tells Yoruba, " 'Mark this night, my Queen of Sheba. And mark my words. I am going to be a great writer one of these days. As soon as I get myself together' " (Killens, 79). Yoruba is fascinated by Lumumba's quick changes in mood. Sensing her warming interest, he recounts his travels, explaining, " 'That's why I've been to all those places, Cairo, Mexico, Brazil. I've just got to find myself. Got to get my thing together' " (Killens, 80). Yoruba comments: " 'You're really trying to escape yourself. You were together when you were up there on the stage doing your thing. But as soon as you put on those dumb glasses and sat at this table, you became someone else. . . . You're with yourself wherever you are, if you're together with yourself. You could be together with yourself right here at this moment, that is, if you would give yourself a chance and get rid of all that excess baggage, all those phoney-baloney other people you've picked up on your way around the world.' " The edifice, always shaky, crumbles. Lumumba speaks "respectfully.

'OOooh! You sure know what to say, Madam philosopher.' Quietly. Smilingly. He shook his head from side to side, no longer smiling. 'I've put on so many masks, sometimes I don't know who I am' " (Killens, 80). The coming together and falling apart of Euro-American symbols has occurred with such frequency and speed that no line of demarcation exists.

In a sense, Lumumba illustrates what happens when the trickster ends by tricking himself. The trickster in Afro-American folklore achieves his ends by manipulating the contradiction between appearance and reality. Functionally, this requires a clear idea of goals and an ability to sense and present the façade the observer wants to see and hear. The shuffling, head-scratching slave may use that pose to hide a perspective and a plan intended to alter the balance of power between slave and master. The trick for the trickster is not to believe his own disguise, and with Yoruba, this is precisely where Lumumba fails.

The cultural baggage that Lumumba has gathered on his various trips is a motley collection over which he exercises imprecise control. He can innocently bring out the wrong piece with ignorant aplomb: a trunk stuffed with ill-suited elegance is produced when an overnight case would do.

Though acute and accurate in her observations, Yoruba sometimes falls prey to the needless vacillation that she condemns in Lumumba. This vacillation is especially intriguing when Lady Daphne discovers that Lumumba and Yoruba have fashioned a relationship.

Lady Daphne asks, referring to Lumumba: " 'Who is that wooly head African? I told you I wanted you to marry a fair-skin colored man, so your children will be lighter than you and have a better chance in life. You're an American.' " To Yoruba's blithe reply that she has no plans for marriage, Lady Daphne assumes that she is "sleeping around" and "living in sin." She concludes in disgust: " 'And they picked you for a debutante.' " But Lady Daphne is not prepared for Yoruba's comeback: " 'Are you going to bring your darling daughter up on charges before the Cotillion Selections Committee?' " Lady Daphne immediately loses all vindictiveness and is embarrassingly understanding. " 'No, child, no! I wouldn't dream of turning you in! I'm your mother through thin and thick' " (Killens, 123). This outpouring of personal concern misses the humorous vein in which Yoruba's question is asked, and, given the exchange's genesis (a too long kiss with a "wooly head African"), it further illustrates the importance that Lady Daphne attaches to the cotillion. Her feelings about Lumumba are a catalyst for several shifts that he and Yoruba attach to personal symbols.

Preparations for the cotillion continue. There are dance lessons taught by a foul-breathed liberal with a lisp, Mr. Phil Potts, "the kind of instructor who could no longer follow his own instructions. Like a five-by-five basketball coach teaching rebounds to Wilt Chamberlin" (Killens, 133). Nevertheless, Mr. Potts does try: " 'Wonth, two, free—Now, ladieth, juth remember—Wonth, two, free—the walth is the—wonth, two, free—take the chewing gum out your mouth—Wonth, two, free—gentility—Wonth, two, free. . . . it is the danth of queens and kings and barons and. . . . all the other people of leisured classes. . . . Oh dear me! That's not quite it. . . . You are funking Broadway [a reference to the "Funky Broadway," a popular dance in the late sixties]—that is not the walth, dearie" (Killens, 129). Charlene Robinson, one of the Harlem "underprivileged" allowed by the Femme Fatales to participate in the cotillion, says of Mr. Potts's attempts. " 'Shee-it! Ain't this a bitch' " (Killens, 130). Several of the other participants laugh.

A series of instructive socials is meant to impart the proper attitude. At one such gathering Mrs. Robinson, determined to discuss a sensitive subject delicately, skates around the topic of sexual intercourse with such airy indirection that all the women are miffed. Mrs. Brap-bap speaks directly, telling the debutantes to keep their "drawers up and their dresses down" until the cotillion is over. The Femme Fatales want to avoid the embarrassment they suffered when several debutantes delivered babies seven months after a previous cotillion. Most attention is paid to selecting an escort. For this there are specific requirements: "The deserving lad should be of superior family background and all that, second-generation Brooklyn at the very least; doctor's, lawyer's, preacher's son. Heir of teacher, celebrity, athlete, postal clerk, and so on. He should be nice looking. Nordically speaking, preferably light skin in coloration, skinny-legged, soft head, on the top. . . . Afros are not smiled on" (Killens, 155).

Lady Daphne lacks the background and money to be a bonafide Femme Fatale, but she clearly embodies their spirit. This is why she is upset when Yoruba announces that Lumumba will be her escort.

" 'He's a wort'less Black woolly-head nigger. . . . Why you ain't like the rest of the young ladies and get yourself a nice boy from the university?' " (Killens, 165). Yoruba attempts to sell Lumumba to her mother. She produces a feature article from the *Amstermdam News* and informs her mother that he has published in the *Black Page, Harlem Journal,* and *Negro Digest.* " 'What do niggers know?' " Yoruba smoothly moves her sales pitch into high gear: " 'He's working on a book, Mother. And his publishers have given him a thousand dollars advance. . . . That's what the story in the *Amsterdam* is all about.' " Lady Daphne pauses. She reasons that white folks do not throw their money away. Perhaps the "woolly-head African" has some redeeming qualities. Her tone softens, " 'If he'd just clean himself up and get a haircut and look like somebody. I've got nothing in my heart against the boy' " (Killens, 168).

Yoruba's residence in her "new Black world" is now more comfortable because her political consciousness is informed by her personal history. Instead of condemning her mother's standards of beauty, she concentrates on something they can agree on. Both are pleased at Lumumba's success, but for different reasons. Lady Daphne becomes flexible because the white world has certified Lumumba, whereas Yoruba's happiness grows from knowledge of the content of his work. Yoruba, in the words of the "New Nationalist," maximizes the positive and minimizes the negative through a form of "operational unity." She is able to do this because her political consciousness has touched ground and intermingled with the specifics of her background. To be sure, both women maintain their individual rationales for accepting Lumumba, and each awaits the opportunity to influence the other. Lady Daphne wants to push Lumumba entirely into the realm of white respectability; Yoruba wants to raise her mother's "black consciousness." Importantly, a line of communication has been established.

The triumphant Yoruba marches off to ask Lumumba to be her escort. His response is an attempt to decide what meaning the cotillion will have. Once asked, he moves from refusal, to fear, to political critique, and finally to acceptance. The movement is initially a function of his immediate state—he is perched on an inaccessible precipice of creative rapture—but it quickly becomes transparent. He wonders if "those empty-headed, Cotillion oriented, glamour-college pretty boys would take" his Yoruba. He quickly turns personal fear into political critique, noting that the Femme Fatales are counterrevolutionary, a sorry "front" organization peddling bad values and incorrect aesthetics to the black community. The word, he tells Yoruba, is "Up the Black Nation"; surely she could see how the cotillion contradicts the "word." Yoruba is saddened by this speech because she knows that on an ideological level Lumumba is correct. Lumumba asks her to drop out of the cotillion. She explains that things have gone too far; her parents have spent money and, she informs him, the cotillion offers a scholarship. Her options are limited, but understanding Lumumba's feelings, she decides to invite someone else to escort her. Lumumba twists and turns away from his ideological correctness because of the simple fact that he loves Yoruba.

Although Lumumba is not an extreme version of the vacillating revolutionary, he does have difficulty separating personal fears from political considerations. This problem is not extraordinary; it becomes so only when exacerbated by extreme fears and needs—a situation that plagued numerous black power advocates. Lumumba's predicament regarding the contradiction between political considerations and personal considerations is crucial in the struggle for self-definition. This predicament was extraordinarily problematic for Afro-Americans during the black power movement because of the difficulty of first defining the meaning of "revolution" in the "freest" country in the world and then trying to implement that definition. The public accommodations and voting rights goals of the civil rights movement had largely been met, leaving the more profound philosophical questions for the black power movement. Its members questioned the extent to which the Judaeo-Christian tradition provided a basis for theorizing black liberation and felt that precedents within African and Afro-American culture held answers to questions of black empowerment.

But parents, family, friends, and lovers were often caught in the old traditions that the black power advocates wanted to change. Profound questions were raised about the role of the black church in the new world, and even such ceremonies as high school graduations had to be invested with a new African spirit. Those who were successful created hybrids, churches, schools, ceremonies, and the like that sought to combine the old with the new. Those who failed shriveled into tight little esoteric circles of ideological clarity and became odd satellites whose orbits took them further and further away from the center of the black community.

What Lumumba and Yoruba share with these black power advocates who were able to combine the old with the new is simple love and respect for black people. I think that those characters who are not successful do not dislike or hate black people; they simply have personal problems—some caused or made worse by racism—which the movement cannot solve.

In deciding to attend the cotillion, Lumumba tells Yoruba, " 'It's just that I love you so.' " Nonetheless, going to the cotillion means following certain rules.

For Lumumba, the meaning of the cotillion as a symbol reflects an uneven mixture of personal and political fears and needs. Because the mixture is not smooth, its components are sometimes antagonistic—a reality that accounts for some of the changes that Lumumba undergoes in the future.

Lumumba is invited to dinner, and Yoruba sees it as an opportunity to show off her African prince and to sway her mother into the realm of black consciousness. Her "New Nationalism" will surely pay dividends. She wears large hoop earrings and a dress of African print. The mood is correct. The doorbell rings, and a neat, smartly dressed black man stands awaiting entrance. He looks familiar, but Yoruba cannot place him. The stranger is a redone Lumumba—hair trimmed, shaved, and wearing a new suit. Lady Daphne is thrilled at the apparent conversion but Yoruba fumes. Dinner is eaten, and Lumumba charms Lady Daphne with his British accent and abundant compliments. They discuss the possibility of revolution in Barbados. " 'There'll never be a revolution in Barbados,' Miss Daphne asserted with finality. 'Ain't you agree?' she demanded of Lumumba" (Killens, 187).

Lumumba feels "Yoruba's angry looks hotly on his face and shoulders." His response is measured: " 'Never is a long time, Miss Daphne. I will say though, there doesn't seem to be any sign of revolutionary fervor in Barbados at this moment.' He mopped his forehead with his handkerchief. Shot a quick glance at Yoruba" (Killens, 187). She can no longer tolerate his performance and informs her mother and father that she and Lumumba are going to a movie.

Yoruba is angered because her plan has foundered. But she has forgotten that in an earlier effort to make Lumumba acceptable to her mother, she too used tactics that had the effect of dulling Lumumba's blackness. Though she saw her tactics as temporary, she does not allow Lamumba this flexibility. She loves him for the quality of his character, but the character must have a certain symbolic appearance to be legitimate; minimally, he needs a large Afro, a beard, and to wear an African garment. Once the couple leaves the house, circumstances corroborate Yoruba's assessment. Lumumba is no longer himself. " 'Who the hell? Do I know you? . . . Brother! That ain't you! Is it? What happened to you baby? . . . You on the stuff? . . . Kick it brother' " (Killens, 189). Lumumba does not have time to react before a group of young black men appears. They "walked up to them with their bad selves with their bad bad walk in their macho bad dashikis. One of them said, 'You ain't Ben Ali Lumumba! Why you shucking and jiving. . . . Another one of the Bloods said, 'We're members of the BBBMF, the Black and Beautiful Bad Mother-Fuckahs. We revolutionaries, baby, and you ain't no Ben Ali Lumumba. He is a swinging ass. He lets it all hang out all over every whichawhere' " (Killens, 193). After some conversation, the BBBMF decide that this "proper looking dude" is Ben Ali Lumumba. "They gave him the shake . . . and strutted up the avenue in their fifty-dollar alligator boots" (Killens, 194).

Situations have been reversed. When Yoruba first met Lumumba his appearance—his clothing as well as his actions—symbolized a black consciousness. This was quickly dashed by his attempts to impress Yoruba by modeling artifacts of Euro-American culture. At Yoruba's home, Lumumba's blackness is more conscious in that it attempts to adjust to the situation; he tries to get close to an elder, even though she is not an ideal model. His appearance at the Lovejoy household suggests a bourgeois consciousness incapable of evolving beyond the necessity of the moment. Actually, as an apparition, the well-groomed Lumumba is continuous with the actions of the apparent "black" Lumumba who spices conversations with superfluous *s'il vous plaîts*. Referring to the shedding of his African appearance, he tells Yoruba: " 'It's nothing but superficial superstructure anyhow. It's a symbol of our Black and beautiful selves, and that's a great thing, but it's not the revolution yet. And cats that don't wear Afros are just as Black and beautiful as them that do' " (Killens, 197). For Lumumba it is a simple question of "tactics not principle." He tells

Yoruba, " 'I'm the same person I was before I went through all those superficial changes' " (Killens, 191).

The scene with the BBBMF causes Lumumba not to desire celebrity status—a position he once craved. He says: " 'They're a half dozen self-anointed glory seeking soothsayers to the block in Harlem, every single one of them saying some jive-ass sooth to their own little separate group of desperate people. . . . Well, that ain't me, Yoruba. . . . I'm not Malcolm's Second Coming. . . . I'm just a cat who's trying to get his thing together. So when I do say something, it will have some small significance for Black people.' " Having made the limitations of hero-worship clear, he says, " 'Damn! I meant to watch Johnny Carson tonight. My main man gon be interviewed. We still got 15 minutes' " (Killens, 195). Lumumba's main man is Jomo Mamadou Zero, a tough-talking militant. Johnny Carson winds up his introduction: ' "Give him a big hand, fellow Americans. He's going to kill every white man in this nation. Bring him out with grand applause. Make this great one feel at home' " (Killens, 198). Zero does not disappoint: " 'I wish all of you pale-face pigs a bad evening, you swinish cannabalistic motherfuckas! And after them few kind words of salutation, I'm going to say one more mean thing to you' " (Killens, 198–99).

Zero's performance caps a bizarre evening. Yoruba is leveled by Lumumba's appearance only to be resurrected to a higher level of political understanding—one she knows and forgets. Lumumba displays the vision and nearsightedness of his political consciousness by first illustrating problems with celebrity status and hero-worship and then running off to see his hero perform. Lumumba and Yoruba can only laugh. "Black folks had to have a sense of humor. Or go out of their minds entirely." Zero's performance is symbolic of his name. The African surnames, Jomo Mamadou, are as Lumumba says of his own attire, superficial superstructure. He concludes: " 'Another man done gone. These goddamn white folks so sophisticated, if they can't beat you, they don't join you, hell naw, they get you to join them. They kiss your damn Black ass to death. . . . No matter what we say to whitey, we always end up his entertainment' " (Killens, 199).

Lumumba's physical metamorphosis and the reaction it caused as well as Jomo Mamadou Zero's performance are remarkable in what they suggest about Afro-American attempts at self-definition during the late sixties and early seventies. For many activists of this era symbols were static and reliable descriptions of people's ideas. In an instructive essay, Richard Long points out some limitations of symbolizing political consciousness: "It is not very likely . . . that generalized beyond a certain number of people they [the various symbolic appearances and actions of sixties activists] were ever much more than a mode of conformity; in other words, a species of fashionable behavior" (Long, 1). Long and others note that many blacks with needs unrelated to specific political thrusts were able to exploit the "conformity" associated with particular appearances to personal gain or simply undercut anything worthwhile about symbolic conformity. This last assertion is illustrated in the novel by the BBBMF, who stroll along in alligator boots, passing out cards that proclaim their availability for revolutionary activity. This cheap advertising reflects poorly on serious political organization.

In *The Cotillion* many of the characters react to Lumumba in the way Richard Long describes, assigning absolute meaning to his appearance: Lumumba the clean-cut is initially invisible to those who know him or think they know him. They respond to appearances in much the same way many Afro-Americans responded to each other during this period. Certain assumptions were immediately made about a black woman who straightened her hair or a black man who wore suits with a European cut. Extreme versions of the latter derided the successful black as a sellout, one out of touch with black reality. To be sure, most members of the black middle class depicted in *The Cotillion* are out of step. Nonetheless, there are exceptions that indicate another tradition. Mrs. Brap-bap and Mrs. Jefferson do not allow success to make them imitate white ritual. The tradition that these two women represent, however, is not the focus of the sixties. A particular appearance indicated a particular consciousness.

Zero's sorry performance illustrates what Herbert Marcuse calls the flattening out of society, the ability of the capitalist system to embrace contradictions without being adversely affected. He writes that the "liquidation of two-dimensional culture takes place not through denial and rejection of 'cultural values,' but through their wholesale incorporation into the established order, through their reproduction and display on a massive scale. . . . If mass communications blend together harmoniously, and often unnoticeably, art, politics, religion, and philosophy with commercials, they bring these realms of culture to their common denominator—the commodity form" (Marcuse, 57). Zero's performance on the "Johnny Carson Show," which is not noted for presenting clarifying social theory, defines the perimeters of the way he can be perceived. He cannot be taken seriously. Like some black activists who, to paraphrase Karenga, shouted *Habari Gani* (what's happening) for the six o'clock news, Zero is entertainment and therefore a digestible commodity for white America. This is certainly the point Lumumba makes.

The juxtaposition of symbols did little to clarify the directions some black organizations took during this period. The strange pictures of Black Panthers in leather jackets standing next to immaculately dressed and smiling white liberals in certain exclusive places in midtown Manhattan, all presumably toasting the coming revolution, suggested different versions of the way the world being fought for might look (Wolfe, 4–5). In this instance, the medium defined the boundaries of the message. Just as Zero was reduced by the "Johnny Carson Show" to mere entertainment, so were the Black Panthers reduced to specimens of primitive revolutionaries who did, after all, know how to hold champagne glasses and make polite conversation. It boggles the mind to imagine what these people had in common and what they talked about.

Lady Daphne faces the reality of her dreamy adulation of whites when she, Yoruba, and Lumumba work as servants at a white cotillion. Yoruba is initially opposed to the idea, and her mother's rationale—that she will be able to see firsthand how whites handle themselves on such occasions—only increases her opposition. She tells Lumumba that she must draw the line, that she compromised herself by agreeing to participate in the cotillion in the first place, and that she will compromise no further. Lumumba is totally comfortable with himself: the earlier militant rhetoric has penetrated his thinking in a fashion that supersedes symbolic correctness. From the flexible wisdom of his maturing consciousness he asks Yoruba: " 'Who're you compromising with? The white power structure whom you despise? Or your mother who birthed you . . . but whom you sometimes disagree with, but whom you love and respect because she is your mother and because she is Black and beautiful whether she wants to be or not?' " (Killens, 224). Yoruba relents, and they all attend the white cotillion as workers.

Lady Daphne moves through three stages at the white cotillion, the last of which desecrates most symbols that she associates with white culture. Lumumba is pleased to exploit the events leading to this point. Lady Daphne wants the whites to know that she understands and appreciates the importance of a cotillion. After all, she is the mother of a debutante. "Lady Daphne went around curtseying respectfully and telling everybody. . . . 'My daughter, the pretty darkskin girl over there, she's going to be in the Grand Cotillion at the Waldorf!' They, the white and proper bourgeois, looked at her as if she had just told them that a donkey had just been ordained for the ministry by the Presbyterian diocese" (Killens, 229). Yoruba has to remind her mother that they are there to work. Lumumba points out the antics of the cotillion participants: " 'Look Miss Daphne, he's goosing her! Isn't that just really the real thing? Look! She's goosing him back! Too much! The really real thing all the way' " (Killens, 232). The cotillion grows increasingly strange. Young men swing Tarzanlike from the chandelier; several couples have an orgy in one of the mansion's dining rooms; others, less bold, content themselves with blowing up prophylactics. Some simply puke away the evening's excess. Lady Daphne tries to ignore these incongruities, but Lumumba is persistent in pointing out each oddity. Several males, drunk and motivated by stereotypical images of easy black women, "move on" Yoruba. Lady Daphne stands guard: "Almost against her will it seemed, her Negritude caught up with her. 'Dance with your own kind, tall drunken gentleman. My daughter is a colored lady' . . . she fought off five or six or seven of the gallant hoodlums of society" (Killens, 240). The accumulation of the evening's events is nightmarish. " 'Let's get out of this God forsaken den of infidels,' " Lady Daphne tells Lumumba. Lady Daphne cannot "stand anymore of these white devils." History has caught her. She can no longer play the bemused and thankful custodian of white genteel society because that society is bestial, without grace or beauty. After this cotillion, Lady Daphne opens herself more fully to her family, admitting that her actions were foolish and motivated by forces alien to her personal and racial history.

Lumumba and Yoruba decide to make the cotillion black by wearing Afros and African attire. They want to make a statement rather than engage in a protracted struggle to "raise the consciousness" of the black middle class. The consciousness of Lumumba and Yoruba has developed to a level that makes it unnecessary to be concerned about what individuals who are not the focus of their actions might think. They know how their decision to make the cotillion black will be seen by the cotillion committee and are therefore unconcerned about how others might feel about their actions. Lumumba and Yoruba have learned to distinguish between appearance and reality. They see the middle class as unrepresentative of the masses and therefore not worth the same level of attention that Lady Daphne receives as a confused member of the masses.

The envelopment of her mind by an alien culture contradicts her personal history and parallels the situation of many blacks in that individuals are socialized to act in a fashion that contradicts personal history and therefore impedes developing racial consciousness. Many initiatives by the cultural nationalists of the sixties were meant to "free the minds" of a captive "Black Nation" (Baraka, Karenga, Madthubuti). The incongruous appearance of Jomo Mamadou Zero on the "Johnny Carson Show" is a fictional reminder that cultural nationalists had little control over the uses to which the symbols they advocated might be put. This is the case with most Afro-American creative efforts: the lack of multinational institutions that can protect, develop, and extend black creativity has meant the constant appropriation of that creativity. The absence of control over the use to which symbols are put trivializes them.

For Richard Long, the notion of black consciousness based on symbolic actions is faulty: "It is my contention that much of what leading spokesmen said or did in the name of black consciousness was either unproductive or counterproductive because of the naivete about symbolizing among the American wing of black diaspora. Further, the avid consumption of symbols by the masses, and black youth particularly, misled certain spokesmen who even today are reeling in disbelief at the collapse of an edifice which was only a facade in the first place" (Long, 1). Symbols associated with black consciousness can project a false sense of development when they lie outside the realm of ideology, organization, and institutionalization. The clean-shaven and neatly dressed Black Muslims of this period were symbolically consistent because they represented a clear ideology and were members of an organization. The Elijah Muhammed–led Black Muslims represented efficiency, self-reliance, and love for black people. Under Muhammed this thrust was consistent. Meanings associated with symbols are most consistent when those symbols are chosen as a result of actions influenced by ideology.

In *The Cotillion,* changes in meanings associated with symbols reflect a character's level of maturation. Lumumba can comfortably alter his appearance when he becomes clear about his goals; that clarity signals the commingling of personal history with political consciousness. Yoruba also becomes less critical of her mother's various bourgeois demands and more diplomatic as her personal history begins to inform her political consciousness. Lady Daphne functions as a caricature and becomes a character only when confronted with the antics of white debutantes and their escorts at the white cotillion. Circumstances force reflection, and humility prevails.

For Lumumba and Yoruba, meanings associated with symbols can be altered when goals are strung together to suggest a philosophical approach to the question of how one who is black is to act and value experience. For these two, symbolic consistency in itself is hollow; the large picture is black unity, and it is more important than various little symbolic quizzes to test one's blackness. Appearances, in any case, do not always correspond to reality. *The Cotillion* asserts that symbolic political activity not directed by goals derived from a clear philosophical framework is often futile and sometimes cruelly humorous. The novel further illustrates that racial love must precede political activity.

References

Baraka, Amiri. *Raise Race Rays Raze.* New York: Random House, 1971.
Cleage, Albert. *The Black Messiah.* New York: Shed and Wand, 1968.
Cleaver, Eldridge. *Soul on Ice.* New York: Dell, 1968.
Gayle, Addison, ed. *The Black Aesthetic.* Garden City, N.Y.: Doubleday, 1971.
Giddings, Paula. *When and Where I Enter: The Impact of Black Women on Race and Sex in America.* New York: Morrow, 1984.
Jones, Leroi, ed. *African Congress.* New York: Morrow, 1972.
Jones, Leroi, and Larry Neal, eds. *Black Fire.* New York: Morrow, 1968.
Karenga, Maulana. "A Strategy for Struggle." *Black Scholar,* November 1973. pp. 8–21.

Killens, John O. *The Cotillion or One Good Bull Is Half the Herd.* New York: Trident Press, 1971.

Lincoln, C. Eric. *Muslims in America.* Boston: Beacon Press, 1961.

Long, Richard. "The Symbolization of Afro-American Culture." CAAS Occasional Paper 12. Atlanta: Center for African and African-American Studies. Atlanta University, n.d.

Madthubuti, Haki. *Enemies: The Clash of Races.* Chicago: Third World Press, 1978.

Marable, Manning. *Blackwater: Historical Studies in Race; Class Consciousness, and Revolution.* Dayton, Ohio: Black Praxis Press, 1981.

Marcuse, Herbert. *One Dimensional Man.* Boston: Beacon Press, 1966.

Muhammed, Elijah. *The Fall of America.* Chicago: Muhammed's Temple of Islam No. 2, 1962.

Napier, George. *Blacker Than Thou.* Berkeley: Eerdman, 1973.

Neal, Larry. "And Shine Swam On." In *Black Fire,* edited by Leroi Jones and Larry Neal. New York: Morrow, 1968. Pp. 638–56.

Randall, Dudley, ed. *The Black Poets.* New York: Bantam Books, 1971.

Wolfe, Tom. *The Electric Kool-Aid Acid Test.* New York: Farrar, Strauss and Giroux, 1968.

9

The Last Days of Louisiana Red:
The HooDoo Solution

Conflicts between and within black power organizations during the sixties that led to racial betrayal, fostered revolutionary nihilism, and deepened problems between black women and men provide the historical context for Ishmael Reed's novel *The Last Days of Louisiana Red.* Like the novelists previously discussed, Reed assumes that solutions to contemporary racial problems lie in the racial past. When characters can appropriate these solutions, they are able to advance the quest for freedom and literacy. The appropriation is accomplished metaphorically through a positive association with Solid Gumbo Works (SGW). As a combination of practicality (literacy) and spirituality (freedom), it is a solution available to all of Reed's characters. SGW serves a role similar to the one served by the black church in *Meridian* and *Look What They Done to My Song.*

Those characters who are not positively associated with SGW lack historical perspective and therefore stumble about, mouthing phrases from ideologies they do not understand and have not meaningfully integrated into their lives. They are nonetheless prepared to attempt to influence individuals and organizations about the correctness of their cause. Because the phrases and slogans common to these characters are grounded in neither personal nor racial history, their activism and their explanations of various events assume a bizarre metaphysical quality: the most brutal and racially destructive acts are justified by a circular logic that condemns all those outside the magic ring. These nihilists do not know, nor do they care to know, of precedents in the Afro-American past; such disinterest is the result of illiteracy. Everything occurs as if for the first time and consequently is unencumbered by precedent. Under these conditions, racial betrayal and nihilistic politics flourish.

An ahistorical perspective also causes problems between black men and women. In the novel the black woman assumes that she is in control of the ideology of an organization and doing what is necessary to improve the lives of Afro-Americans. In the shadows is a shrewd white man who manipulates the black woman into a mode of thinking that obscures historical precedent. Sometimes knowingly but more often unknowingly, the black woman conspires with the white man to keep the black man in his place—which is any number of stereotypes that emphasize ignorance, incompetence, and irresponsibility as the dominant characteristics of the black man. This primitive, who only recently crawled from the realm of the semiconscious into the light of full consciousness, is a great lover and athlete, for the animal instincts have not been diminished by the march of civilization.

The particular brand of historical ignorance that troubles Reed's characters is called "Louisiana Red." All the characters—good and bad—have been influenced by this disease. It adapts to its environment and to its historical period: "When Osiris entered Egypt, cannibalism was in vogue. Thousands of years later when Ed Yellings entered Berkeley, there was a plague too, but not as savage. After centuries of learning how to be subtle, the scheming beast that is man had acquired the ability to cover up. When Ed Yellings entered Berkeley . . . men were inflicting psychological stress on one another. Driving one another to high blood pressure, hardening of the arteries, which only made matters worse, since the stabbings, rapings, muggings went on as usual. Ed Yellings, being a Worker, decided he would find some way to end Louisiana Red, which is what all this activity was called" (Reed, *Red*, 6). Ed's cure, SGW, is never precisely defined. It needs to be as dynamic and flexible as the disease it is intended to cure. Indeed, as a combination of spirituality and practicality, or as indicated above, as a combination of freedom and literacy, it cannot be precisely defined; rather, SGW is to be understood as a process. Additionally, given the propensity of the Moochers—the antagonistic organization in the novel—to attempt to co-opt or destroy that which they do not understand, it is necessary for SGW to be fluid. In many ways, as a process, SGW is as improvisational as the lives of Afro-Americans. Wrestling with life's constraints and opportunities in an environment that routinely limits the material acquisitions necessary to self-determination in a commodity-driven society demands that Afro-Americans be creative in all spheres of life.

Before discussing how the themes of this novel help us to understand some aspects of the black power movement, I must first analyze the aesthetic framework that influences the direction the novel takes. Reed, much more than the other novelists I have dealt with, has written a great deal about the aesthetic that directs his work. Obviously, his aesthetic accounts for the novel's point of view and for its organization. Reed labels his aesthetic "Neo-HooDoo": "Neo-HooDoo believes that every man is an artist and every artist is a priest. You can bring your own creative ideas to Neo-HooDoo. Charlie Yardbird (Thoth) Parker is an example of Neo-HooDoo artist as an innovator and improviser" (Reed, *Conjure,* 25). The literary applications of Neo-HooDoo are capable of everything: "Fantasy, Nationalism, the supernatural, Hoodism, realism, Science Fiction, autobiography, satire, scat, Eroticism, Rock, K.C. Blues. Intrigue and Jazz" (Reed, *Conjure,* 26). The combinations of these different ways of conceiving and presenting reality distort our sense of what is and what is not fiction, thereby creating interesting questions of verisimilitude. Could world history have evolved, as Reed asserts in *Mumbo Jumbo,* around the struggles between secret societies to gain ascendancy? And could the battle between Set and Osiris be the meaningful historical conflict that explains contemporary contradictions between scientific and intuitive paradigms? For the purposes of my study, finding answers to these questions is not as important as raising the questions. The second question leads to alternative interpretations of white reactions to the black arts movement, especially that movement's righteous decision to discard perceived Euro-American cultural artifacts and replace them with perceived African and Afro-American artifacts. The philosophical result was to reverse ways of interpreting reality, particularly the castigation of sterility and coldness associated with perceived white scientific paradigms. The black man, according to black arts advocates, is natural man—a designation meant to indicate an innate spirituality and practical harmony with one's environment that, though underdeveloped through miseducation, could be reclaimed. Although this "natural man" designation bore surface similarity to existing stereotypes of blacks as brutes or barely articulate animals, the image, like the proclamation "Black Is Beautiful," actually reversed meanings previously associated with the respective images. The "natural man" was projected as the ideal to which civilization strove so as to make life fully integrated and meaningful. The literary applications of the Neo-HooDoo aesthetic can be extended into the real world to provide new interpretations of particular historical events.

Reed uses his aesthetic to retrieve the most esoteric aspects of African and world history and to fuse them with contemporary events. The result is necromancy that has broad explanatory powers. The combination of objective and imaginative events and analyses indicates that no one way of knowing has *a priori* precedence over another. As was the case in Ellington's jazz aesthetics in *Tragic Magic,* a combination of temperament and situation dictates the expression of feeling and thought at a given moment.

In *The Last Days of Louisiana Red,* Gumbo is the meaningful metaphor, the specific structural expression of Neo-HooDoo. The novel, like Gumbo, is "an exquisite and delicious" combination of literary and folkloristic forms. Several of the chapters are presented as a playwright might: the scene is set and characters are allowed to speak without authorial intrusion. A stream-of-consciousness technique is used sparingly to allow access to the innermost thoughts of Street, Minnie, and Max. Reed uses a character named Chorus to provide historical commentary for Minnie's actions. A constant and brilliant connection is made between setting and action. The former is an actual physical and spiritual space, providing its inhabitants with certain constraints and opportunities. The duplicity and arrogance of Maxwell Kasavubu correspond to his New York City origins. Ed Yellings's violent death in Berkeley, given its "rough-and-tumble" history as a cowtown populated by unsophisticated "heavies," is perfectly understandable.

The blending of myths and history and the use of characters from other fictions function in *The Last Days of Louisiana Red* to help clarify the meanings of the upheavals of the sixties for Afro-American activists. The relationship of Minnie and Street with other characters, as well as with SGW, suggests meanings for intraracial strife resulting from organizational expressions of different ideologies. The solutions that characters positively associated with SGW offer to end the strife will illustrate the theme found in all the novels treated here—the turning to aspects of Afro-American history for the understanding and direction needed to advance the quest for freedom and literacy. These characters' responses, especially their decision to decentralize SGW, can be seen as a metaphoric solution to problems of infiltration and loss of community control that plagued some black organizations during the sixties. Within the context of racial betrayal, revolutionary nihilism, and problems between black women and men, Reed's novel explores the way individuals advanced or did not advance the quest for freedom and literacy during the sixties.

The characters in *The Last Days of Louisiana Red* do not develop through either sudden or gradual realizations of their place in a historical tradition. Hewn as they are from Reed's Neo-HooDoo paradigm, they illustrate the results of adhering to one set or another of "loas" (spirits). The Moochers worship destructive loas, and the characters who are positively associated with SGW worship creative loas. Characters in the former group must be brought to understanding in pre- or extralogical ways. It takes divine intervention to make Minnie aware of positive aspects of Afro-American history; more specifically, it takes divine intervention for this even to exist. Reed's concerns are epic; the characters are in some way the sport of the gods. Given Reed's aesthetic, an analysis of their interactions with regard to racial betrayal, revolutionary nihilism, and black male/female relationships enables one to derive meanings that the sixties had for blacks who were politically active.

Racial betrayal in *The Last Days of Louisiana Red* is inflamed by Moocher activity:

> Moochers are people who, when they are to blame, say it's the other fellow's fault for bringing it up. . . . Moochers ask you to share when they have nothing to share. . . . Moochers talk and don't do. You should hear them just the same. Moochers tell other people what to do, men Moochers blame everything on women. Women Moochers blame everything on men. Moochers think it's real hip not to be able to read and write. Like Joan of Arc the arch witch, they boast of not knowing A from B. . . . Though Moochers wrap themselves in the full T-shirt of ideology, their only ideology is Mooching. . . . Moochers inject themselves between the poor and what other people who are a little better off than the poor set aside for the poor.

. . . Moochers feel that generosity should flow one way: from you to them. If you call a Moocher wrong, he'll say: "I'm not wrong, you're paranoid." Freud gave Moochers their greatest outs. Moochers talk so much about "integrity" when in fact they lead scattered ragged lives. Moochers are predators at the nesting grounds of industry. Moochers decided to start an organization themselves. (Reed, *Red,* 17–18)

The Moochers give irresponsibility an aesthetic appeal by draping it in dazzling ambiguities that ignore history. This way the Moochers seem not only correct but inevitable, a manifest destiny of roaring ignorance. Their lack of historical perspective is tantamount to illiteracy. As noted earlier, it is precisely the lack of historical consciousness and an advancement of spontaneity over well-planned tactics that create the ideal conditions for racial betrayal.

Conspirators and coconspirators work to hinder the development of a historical consciousness among the various characters. The conspirators are Maxwell Kasavubu, Nanny Lisa, and T Feeler. The coconspirators are never fully aware of their role; they too are manipulated by whites. Minnie is the primary coconspirator, and she is used by Kasavubu and his people to subvert the dominant manifestation of self-determining activity among Afro-Americans, SGW.

As Moocher president, Minnie gives speeches that are a mixture of slogans drawn from disparate ideological areas that end up as a convoluted intellectualism that numbs her audience. She explains politics to her sister: " 'O Sister, you're so dense. You know I was always the one in the family who was good for theory. . . . LaBas [a HooDoo detective from New York sent to solve the murder of Minnie's father, Ed Yellings] and your kind will be locked in interminable struggle against the fascist insect! It's inevitable' " (Reed, *Red,* 57). Sister complains, " 'There you go . . . Minnie talk. . . . It sounds the same whoever says it. Who says everything has to be that way?' " (Reed, *Red,* 57–58). Minnie responds distantly: " 'My slogans. . . . They tell me. My slogans know everything. With my slogans I can change the look of the future anytime I wish . . . now with my slogans we're able to match wits with the best of them. All this, due to our slogans. My slogans be praised' " (Reed, *Red,* 58). Minnie's slogans are vague because they lack a historical dimension.

Minnie's speeches become so obtuse that the Moocher Board of Directors considers replacing her. Cinnamon Easterhood, the *Moocher Monthly* editor, protests: " 'The sister has a fine mind. . . . She's

writing an article in the *Moocher Monthly* magazine on the mor-
phological, ontological and phenomenological ramifications in
which she will refute certain long held contradictory conclusions
commonly held by peripatetics entering menopause. Why the dialec-
tics of the—' " (Reed, *Red,* 72). Moocher Board of Directors member
Big Sally is unimpressed with the utility of Minnie's "fine mind":—
" 'We don't need no ontology, we need some grits, and Minnie ain't
bringin no grits. Ain't no ontology gone pay our light bill. P.G. and
E. fixin to cut off our Oakland Office. Disconnect. We need somebody who knows how to get down' " (Reed, *Red*, 78). Minnie's
unintegrated intellectualism is incapable of fulfilling the "get down"
imperative.

Sister makes a similar point when she observes that Minnie
" 'needs to get out more. Party some. They're beginning to call her,
well . . . cold. Her own Minnies say she puts them to sleep' " (Reed,
Red, 58). Minnie's lack of success in her writing and speeches results
from her failure to acknowledge the complexities of the Afro-American experience. She focuses only on the fact of oppression, which she
uses as a basis for comparing the Afro-American experience with that
of other Third World people who have been or are oppressed. Shared
oppression becomes the basis for theories of revolution which, inten-
tionally or not, cloud and finally deny the uniqueness of the Afro-
American experience. The same reductionism was practiced by some
black power advocates who advanced Marxist and in some cases
nationalist interpretations of the Afro-American experience (Salaam,
Madthubuti).

The most primitive of the Marxists' interpretations assume a
religious quality. One had only to believe certain basic tenets—for
example, that class, not race, determined consciousness—and then
everything concerning revolutionary change would fall into logical
order. The aim was to teach people how they should feel and act in the
world based on their class affiliation. In making these assertions,
black Marxists gave only passing consideration to the role of the
media in shaping consciousness. It did not occur to them that the
pervasive influence of the media might have permanently altered the
way people, particularly workers—the social agents for change—
perceived of reality and therefore their relationship to it. Any revolutionary role the worker might play in redistributing wealth had to
take account of the influence of the media. This theory is not new, but

it certainly did not animate the thinking of many black Marxists during the sixties.

The ahistorical nature of black Marxists' approach creates a more powerful void in their argument. By the sixties it should have been clear that Marxist theory was not sufficient to direct social change in Afro-America and in America generally, and it certainly should have been clear that various Marxist organizations were so riddled with racism and chauvinism that they were unable to motivate the masses of black people to social change.

In some ways, the black Marxists' assumptions resemble those of Truman Held and Lynne Rabinowitz in Walker's *Meridian* and of Antar in McCluskey's novel. None of these characters has genuine respect for black people. They do not see the institutions that have provided a basis for black survival and development as capable of being extended and made useful to meet new challenges. Rather, the institutions—particularly the black church but any institution with a clear nationalist orientation—are seen as impediments to moving into a colorless society. Indeed, it became fashionable to refer to nationalists as "narrow nationalists" or as chauvinists. These are remarkable accusations to level at members of a race who have systematically been brutalized because of their color. Further, there is little in American or world history to suggest that black attitudes toward whites hindered the march into a colorless society. The opposite is clearly the case.

The reductionism associated with the nationalists usually resulted from a "black" version of the ideas that led Minnie the Moocher to such bizarre activity. Like Minnie they wanted a level of clarity and purity relative to Afro-American life that could be obtained only through idealization. Usually when African history was idealized, any African complicity in the slave trade was minimized or ignored. Various cultural customs, particularly those associated with diet and relationships between black women and men, were also idealized. Increasingly, diets had to be purged of all synthetic foods and, in some nationalist organizations, women were largely reduced to having babies for the revolution.

In its specific applications, the nationalist reductionism, unlike the Marxist reductionism of the era, did share an unpleasant tendency with the Marxist in its castigation and denial of the methods and institutions that Afro-Americans had built over time to deal with their problems. In gross instances, the black church was seen only as an enslaving institution, guaranteed to keep blacks dissatisfied. The NAACP and the Urban League, despite impressive legislative victories, were seen as "Uncle Tom" institutions of little use to the coming revolution. They were clearly not "black enough."

It is notable that despite the pulls from the Left via some black Marxists and from the Right via some black nationalists, the black church remains a focal point of social change. Politicians of all races and political persuasions who wish to influence blacks must still make the obligatory appearance at the black church.

Although both black nationalists and black Marxists were guilty of historical reductionism, the black Marxist approach strikes me as the more illiterate because its philosophical underpinnings are in conflict with the historical Afro-American conception of reality. Specifically, Afro-American life illustrates that consciousness determines being much more than being determines consciousness. Faith, which is a sublime expression of consciousness, has been the motivating force in most struggles for Afro-American self-determination. On one level, this was necessary because of the limited opportunities that our objective conditions have dictated. But on another and perhaps more profound level, African and Afro-American history illustrates that consciousness expressed as faith is a greater determinant of our actions than are material conditions. Afro-Americans, like other ethnic groups, are more than the results of either material conditions or oppression. The dialectic between objective and subtle subjective forces that operates in the lives of all people was often denied Afro-Americans by their fellows who espoused Marxist ideology. All of a sudden, Afro-Americans were mute matter, without a vibrant and resilient culture capable of adapting to, dealing with, or transcending that special area of opportunity that exists at the intersection of objective situation and racial (or personal) history. Afro-Americans have consistently had to draw on pre– or extralogical forms of knowing to gain energy and direction for their struggles to change society. How, then, could anyone hoping to animate the masses of Afro-Americans dismiss those systems as anachronistic or useless?

The black Marxist has found a limited audience in his community primarily because his version of reality is too gross, attempting to attribute people's mentality to objective conditions. For the masses of Afro-Americans, racism and its attendant applications cannot be fully explained from a materialist perspective. Such an assertion will not move the the people very far. Similarly, Minnie's profusely researched abstractions succeed only in putting "her own Minnies" to sleep.

In *The Last Days of Louisiana Red* and among some sixties activists who advanced Marxist interpretations, the conditions for racial betrayal were in place because of a lack of historical understanding. This absence is tantamount to illiteracy and explains why the masses in the world and the majority of the characters in the novel do not follow the leaders in question here. Not knowing that the philosophical framework from which her demands flow is antithetical to black needs, Minnie assumes that she is working for her people. She attempts to convince Street to make SGW "go public":

> [Street] "I'm going to work with this Max.
> That's what I'm going to do."
> [Minnie] "But when I tell him you are cynically using this organization to further your ends—"
> [Street] "Max is with me. He ain't up here in Berkeley for no Moochers. He's up here for another reason. . . . That man is from New York. New Yorkers don't believe in anything. They like crows. . . . They size up a situation and see what they can get from it. . . . It's people in the sticks like you believe in things." (Reed, *Red*, 92)

In unmasking Kasavubu's motives, Street leaves Minnie without her most precious possession—a perceived mastery of explanatory theory. She is proven to be exactly what she accuses Sister of being—"dense." Because her commitment is an emotional one caused by "Louisiana Red," she is uninterested in new information, particularly when that new information suggests that things are not as they appear to be. Minnie sees SGW—which symbolizes the practical and spiritual dimensions of literacy—as a possible cure. Her ignorance causes her to betray blacks by attempting to destroy organizational efforts that grow from philosophies other than the one to which she adheres.

This tendency was evidenced in the sixties, sometimes violently, but more frequently in heated exchanges, which often were mutual condemnations that lacked historical perspective. There were notable exceptions—the National Black Political Conventions held in Gary, Indiana, and Little Rock, Arkansas, are exemplary—that attempted to fuse efforts that grew from different ideologies. These efforts were certainly more constructive than were narrow attempts at ideological clarity.

The Moocher Board of Directors agrees that Minnie "ain't bringing no grits" and decides that Kasavubu should fly to Africa to offer the Moocher leadership to Street. Street's acceptance of the job does not signal a more sophisticated level of political understanding within the Moocher organization than existed under Minnie's leadership. Minnie calcifies audiences with studied ambiguities, and Street enlivens them with colorful, though equally ambiguous, political rhetoric. For both function within the nebulous boundaries of the Moocher organization, which are continualy redrawn, not by principle but by expediency and the desire to be rid of SGW, to be rid of historically based racial understanding. Minnie's muddled intellectualism represents one way of organizing black needs and desires, and Street's "bad nigger" radicalism represents another. Without historical understanding both approaches are only ego expanders.

Kasavubu explains why the Moochers, indeed, why the country, need Street:

> In these times when things are so structured, so sterile, people need someone to remind them of the power of spontaneity, of uninhibited existential action.
> . . . When you used to come into those parties in those high heels, those floppy three-musketeers' hats, those earrings you wore and that headrag. That headrag all greasy and nasty. . . . People would say, Now there goes someone who is just like a natural man. Then, that night, you came into that party with nothing but those gold chains on you, symbolizing the dreaded past, and that Isaac Hayes haircut. You remember Street? . . . The people bought it. (Reed, *Red*, 80)

The masses are seen as wanting a colorful performer, an irresponsible type plucked from the core of the "lumpen." Such a hero would touch their hearts through fashion and rhetoric. The accuracy of this perception aside, Street and Kasavubu decide that an essentially destructive philosophy can be sufficiently disguised to be something other than itself and therefore appear as exactly what the people want and need. Certainly Kingfish and Brown feel that Street's antics are what the people need. They discuss Street's way of handling conflict:

> *Kingfish:* (mimicking gesture) No, the nigger say, "Excuse me, that seat is reserved for me." Next thing they know that nigger was holding his brains in. . . .

Brown: Yeah, that was something. Look like chittlins coming out.

Kingfish: (tears of laughter) Street told the nigger we don't believe in no reserved. We Moochers believe that niggers—all of them— is in the same boat. (Reed, *Red,* 48)

This destructive spontaneity is what Moochers want. When seen through the fictive prism of *The Last Days of Louisiana Red* the incidence of black on black crime ceases to be merely a function of responding to and in some cases attempting to transcend the constraints of white society. In the world of this novel, the simple designation "victims of society" does not fully explain the cruelty of Kingfish, Brown, and Street. Several of the respondents in John Gwaltney's important book *Drylongso* make the same point. Essentially, they say that there are some bad black folks who have to be run out of the community so that the majority of the inhabitants can live safely.

Street's leadership of the Moochers is pure showmanship. He has no delusions about undertaking political reform. He explains to Minnie what moves the masses: " 'Do you know what people want? They want lots of blood; monkeys roller skating; 200 dwarfs emerging from a Fiat, and lots of popcorn—that's what they want. Scorn you when you alive, but if you die—a hero's funeral. The people gobble up anything in the limelight and then ask for seconds. That's the people. Do you think the people like to hear about issues you bring up? You load them down with issues—free this, free that, Algeria, Bulgaria, the principality of Diptheria, buttons, slogans and posters. The people hate that shit' " (Reed, *Red,* 90–91). Street's mesmerizing style is like a series of flashbulbs exploding one after the other. Pyrotechnic leadership is glamorous and limits the need to obtain literacy. For literacy would preclude the speed that obfuscating performances require. Media attention during the sixties furthered the equating of leadership with showmanship, and some activists simply performed.

This approach was particularly easy because of the symbolization of the black power movement, an issue discussed in the previous chapter. Blackness was reduced to a formula as predictable as the "sitcom" or the soap opera, which made it possible for any number of "spokesmen" to stand in front of whites and decry racism and champion their special versions of blackness. Some of these people were able to generate income by manipulating and extending the symbols. The symbolization of the struggle and the inability of black organizations to control the meaning and dissemination of those symbols reduced the black struggle for self- determination to its least common denominator, that of a commodity.

In *The Last Days of Louisiana Red,* racial betrayal is a function either of political activity that lacks a historical base or of simple opportunism. Knowledge is the cure for the former; Reed seems to suggest annihilation of the opportunists. The Streets of the black community are beyond redemption. This part of the novel is in keeping with the militant aspects of the black power movement as well as the perspective of the average black woman and man. Many of the respondents in Gawltney's *Drylongso* make the point that the dope peddlers, prostitutes, and pimps of the black community are unsavable and should be jailed indefinitely.

The Moochers' advocacy of ahistorical political activity and opportunism creates a revolutionary nihilism that obviates political victory by advocating spontaneous violence. Minnie persuades Street to confront their brother Wolf and Papa LaBas relative to SGW's financial success. Minnie reasons that Street deserves a share of the profits by virtue of family relationship. As usual, Minnie has ulterior motives. Street goes along with the plan's stated rationale and appeals to Wolf's recollection of the "good old days": " 'Hey, man. This is me Wolf. This is your brother Street. Remember when we used to go to parties together? All the girls we used to take up to Grizzly Park. . . . Wolf you got to go with me, your brother' " (Reed, *Red,* 98). This melodrama is intended to isolate Papa LaBas and to put SGW solidly under the Yellings's control—a precondition for Street's ultimate takeover. Wolf neatly deflates Street's bubbly sincerity by placing it in an appropriate context: " 'We're grown now, Street. . . . Our family has had its share of bad troubles. But now, for the first time, with LaBas at the helm, I feel that things don't have to be so accursed. It's not fate that's holding us back. We just have to learn how to cut it, Street; that's what LaBas has taught me. . . . All you knew how to do was to destroy. Maybe destruction was good then, it showed our enemies we meant business. But we can't continue to be kids burning matches when the old folks are away. We have to buckle down' " (Reed, *Red,* 98–99). Wolf wants Street to pull himself up so as to create instead of destroy.

The twisted Moocher ideology gives Street's ignorance and opportunism a voice and justifies intraracial violence. Wolf pleads, "We don't need bloodshed," and Street responds, " 'We do! We always need bloodshed! You can see the blood dripping. It's both immediate and symbolic, it moves people. . . . You two [Wolf and LaBas] have to work year around to get results; all I have to do is cut swiftly, accurately, and people will see what I mean' " (Reed, *Red,* 99). Though actions may well speak louder than words, their meaning is not always clear because they are motivated by ahistorical Moocherism. Moocher political activity has a bizarre nihilistic quality because it denies the Afro-American experience any acknowledged place in the formation and implementation of theory. Systematic analysis is unnecessary when one need only cut "swiftly" and "accurately." Street's spontaneous bloodlust leads to a revolutionary nihilism that has parallels in contemporary history.

Various black activists of the sixties felt or expressed the idea that suicidal activity had useful political dimensions. In fact, Huey Newton's book is titled *To Die for the People.* I do not mean to question the sincerity of Newton or any other black leader who had similar sentiments, but I believe their activism often lacked an affecting historical foundation and their theories tended to be so eclectic that almost any tactic, from "offing the pig" to "dying for the people" had the same utility.

Another consequence of the Moochers' ahistorical character is the idea that racial progress inevitably involves bloodletting. Moochers are adamant in their quest to root out, expose, and destroy all "bushwa niggers." This designation applies to all blacks who are self-reliant and who work from a black perspective. Andy and Kingfish discuss past victories:

> *Kingfish:* You remember the time we took over the Black Studies Program up here Andy?
> *Brown:* Yeah, I remember it. We bopped the bushwa nigger who was running it, and he had a big hickey on his head. Then we took over.
> *Kingfish:* Those was the days, Andy, the sixties. They took us off television and the radio and gave us freedom to roam the world, unchecked, hustling like we never hustled before. (Reed, *Red,* 118)

The hapless Black Studies director is not as fortunate as his real-life contemporaries who, though criticized, were not bopped on the head. Often blacks in professional positions were the recipients of verbal abuse which questioned their goals and intentions in any given instance (Hare). Similarly, several black organizations purged their ranks of bourgeois individuals who displayed liberal tendencies (Madthubuti, "Latest Purge"). They did so when some nationalists became Marxists (Madthubuti, "Enemy"). They seldom questioned the legitimacy of the categories used to codify blacks as bourgeois or revolutionary. Numerous references were made to black African thinkers who used Marxist thought to direct their struggles for independence, but the result was reductionist because no effort was made to indicate and deal with differences between socioeconomic conditions in black Africa and in black America (Baraka, "Need"; Karenga). As when any shift in ideology and tactics occurs, positive and negative attributes are revealed. The rapid move by some activists from a nationalist to a Marxist perspective was precipitated less by the failure of nationalist actions than by the activists' internal needs. Given the incredible odds against any black woman or man who struggles with others of like mind in an attempt to alter the course of history, it is more than understandable why some nationalist activists may have grown tired. The level of intensity under which they worked could not be maintained. In reaching these conclusions, my assumption is that America remains a conglomeration of competing ethnic groups and that for any group to rise it must develop and maintain its own culture. As Cruse and others have pointed out, America is not a melting pot but a pluralistic society in which race remains a primary determinant of action and opportunity.

The effective dimension between Minnie and some sixties activists is similar: useful political organizations and coalitions were dismantled by individuals who were ignorant of history, simply opportunistic, or some combination of both. Minnie's decision to work for the release of Kingfish and Andy from prison—the two are caught in the act of robbing a friend's home—is illustrative of political activity gone amuck. She explains her latest cause: " 'The brothers were unjustly busted in the home of one of LaBas's workers. The corrupt bushwa is some kind of double agent because he called the police on his brother' " (Reed, *Red,* 174). Kingfish and Andy, like Street, are given the unjustified designation of political prisoners.

Passing out leaflets to inform passersby about the two "political prisoners" is not enough for Minnie; she becomes ensnarled in the correctness of her case and initiates direct action: "About an hour ago Minnie busted George Kingfish Stevens and Andy Brown out of jail and then commandeered an airplane after miraculously evading San Francisco security, which was as tight as a drum" (Reed, *Red,* 156). Moocherism makes suicidal activity, which in this instance lacks a moral basis (the men are thieves), triumphantly political. Minnie will gladly die for the people—even if the people are not terribly interested in what she fights for.

Minnie's desire to be a strong leader in the tradition of Marie Laveau and Antigone creates problems between black women and men similar to those that existed within the black community during the sixties. She is a feminist politician of the worst variety, who, like Laveau, uses spies and innuendo to realize her goals. Minnie also has Laveau's insatiable ego, which will tolerate no power other than her own. Like Antigone, Minnie is a complainer and a manipulator who is given to periodic outbursts against cruel fate, although she does strike out against fate when victory is certain. Throughout the melodrama—the recoiling and repulsion in reaction to fate and the needless rending of garments—Minnie manages to ignore the fact that the struggle exists only in her snarled consciousness. As suggested earlier, it is this confusion—initiated by Kasavubu—that blocks her development. Papa LaBas attempts to point out the alliance between black women and white men: " 'Oh, you're denying the very lucrative benefits that go along with being a black woman in a white man's country? One of our Business people, Zora Neale Hurston, had an informant in Georgia say, "White men and black women are running this thing." ' " (Reed, *Red,* 127). Minnie does not believe this, so LaBas provides further evidence: " 'When Governor Earl Long made a speech before the Louisiana Legislature about its existence, he was put into an asylum for giving away the Brotherhood. . . . But now the old lovers [black women and white men] have entered into a conspiracy to put the negro male into the kitchen and to death' " (Reed, *Red,* 129).

LaBas is not only criticizing a perspective that deemphasizes the role of the black man, he is also giving that deemphasis a historical basis: "You can find many examples of cooperation culled from slave narratives, old newspapers, family records and other documents found in North and South America" (Reed, *Red,* 128). LaBas assigns black women a level of free choice that, considering the circumstances of slavery, seems curious. LaBas makes his claims to correct what Reed sees as the unfair treatment that black men have received (Reed *Conjure*, 136). He wants the record to acknowledge those black men who made the best of a bad situation. It is more reasonable to argue that black women during the sixties were able to exercise free choice than to say they did so in the slave era.

The "kitchen" to which LaBas accuses Minnie of wanting to condemn the black man is a monolith of stereotypes that seem lifted from random perceptions that whites have of blacks. LaBas complains to Minnie: " 'You and your roustabouts and vagrants just couldn't stand negro men attempting to build something; if we were on the corner sipping Ripple, then you would love us, would want to smother us with kindness' " (Reed, *Red,* 125). The operative stereotype is "a nigger ain't shit." LaBas and the others who are positively associated with SGW violate this stereotype and must be forced back into their assigned roles. After Minnie's feeble objection to the above observation—" 'That's not the truth,' " she says—LaBas continues: " 'It's the truth. It's been the truth since we were enslaved into being the same—hammered into the same and kept there by white and negro forces. Every fool the same as a wise man, griot or warrior. The philosophy of slavery—the philosophy of inferiority' " (Reed, *Red,* 125). The reductionist logic of Moocherism that LaBas criticizes is a parody of some black Marxists who advance the interpretations of reality that place people in categories purely on the basis of objective conditions, especially their relationship to the means of production (Walters). Being a black male in America has meant unrelenting oppression and a circumscribed existence that militates against even partial self-realization. Such a man must turn to drink or mayhem for solace. Both the black Marxists and the Moochers see objective conditions as determiners of consciousness. Thus, to paraphrase LaBas, the simple fact of being black is enough to make every man—fool, griot, or wise man—the same.

Whether from ignorance or by choice, the result of the alliance between the black woman and the white man is destructive to the black man. If intelligent, he is castigated for being "uppity," not knowing his place. If dull or slow, he is coddled and further underdeveloped. In either case, Moocher ideology will not allow the black man full humanity.

Minnie has other stereotypes at her disposal that are periodically unfurled to justify her claim to leadership. One is the long–suffering black woman. Minnie claims: " 'The sisters have been wronged, and it is time for us to take over; we've held the family together for all these years' " (Reed, *Red,* 128). This stereotype of the black matriarch is followed, if not supported, by the stereotype of the irresponsible black male. " 'It's the negro man who is to blame. He's like an insect that fertilizes a woman and then deserts her. All he knows is basketball and pussy' " (Reed, *Red,* 129). With these arguments stitched loosely together, Minnie feels qualified to lead. The black man, after all, has had his chance and has proven himself embarrassingly inept. Minnie, however, loses the Moocher leadership to Street and therefore must resort to indirect methods to obtain her goals:

> [Street]. "You're my sister, all right. Scared to get fucked. Scared to do anything. Trembling. Whatever gave you the right to think you could lead a man!"
> [Minnie] "I'm qualified. . . ."
> [Street] "Qualified. Qualified for what! To talk theory. Talking a lot of shit. You sound stupid. You better try and get you some dick and take your mind off this bullshit." (Reed, *Red,* 89–90).

The feminist Minnie is insulted by this crass transformation of a political discussion into a sexual need.

Street's direct assault does provide insight into the sexual politics of the sixties. His advice—"try and get you some dick"—is a crude version of the sixties "have a baby for the revolution" school of thought. This slogan, like others associated with the black power movement, ran the risk of being exploited by individuals who had decidedly limited perspectives. A legitimate concern with genocide through various forms of birth control was perverted by many to justify sexual relations. The concern became just one more way to "bed" a sister.

Street wants Minnie to leave the frigid zone of her theoretical politics and have some fun; indeed, Sister has the same advice for Minnie. Although Street's solution to Minnie's cold, manipulative, and humorless character has some legitimacy, that solution, by extension, is clearly debilitating to black women. All the political activities of black women that appear confused and self-defeating are not a function of sexual frustration.

In *The Last Days of Louisiana Red,* the problems between black women and men are like all the problems these characters experience; they result from a confluence of arrogance and historical ignorance. Minnie does not know that she is being manipulated by a white man; she therefore feels confident in asserting the correctness of her analysis of black female and male relationships. That this analysis is a simple collection of stereotypes escapes Minnie. Because Reed is concerned with balancing the record, the black man is not seen as an equal partner with his mate in the creation of problems. Street engages in random carnage and chauvinism, but his character is not developed with the same concern for historical precedent that typifies Minnie's development. Street is simply a bad seed grown into a malevolent hybrid that can be bent around any sick desire. The attempts of Minnie, as an ignorant inheritor of "Louisiana Red"–infected aspects of Marie Laveau and Antigone, to manipulate the black male are catastrophic.

As indicated earlier, SGW is a metaphoric reification of spiritual and practical aspects of Afro-American history. Its reorganization at the end of the novel is instructive for understanding ways that some black organizations were infiltrated and destroyed during the sixties and how those same organizations could have saved themselves. After Street and Wolf mistakenly kill each other—an indirect result of Minnie's scheming—Minnie confronts LaBas, demanding that SGW be given to her as an inheritance. LaBas explains:

> "We're phasing out. . . . You see, as long as we're conspicuous, as long as we're in the public's eye with a definable point of operation, there will be scandals, murder. As long as we're trying to take care of Business, people like you will always seek us out and attempt to enervate us. Without a central location, if we're inaccessible, beyond reach, we'll be more able to devote our full energy to the work, communicating with each other only when the need arises. The competition would rather have us on the public dole than let us achieve anything and they use people like you to keep it that way and to inhibit the development of our quality." (Reed, *Red*, 124)

This is a masterful rendering of both the problems that many black organizations face as well as the solution to those problems. Blacks' attacks on their own organizations is the first problem, but the motivation for such attacks did little to change their destructive consequences. The second problem is co-optation by the larger society—that sorry performance of Jomo Mamadou Zero in Killens's novel—and the subsequent transformation of symbols. The cutthroat Street can spit up never-digested slogans and be considered a leader, a credit to his race. Similarly, the frenetic Minnie dashes about destroying much of what she touches. Failing intragroup rivalry, cooptation, and the subsequent transformation of symbols, the larger society can create scandals or murder those resistant to such activity.

SGW is subjected to all of the above but manages to survive because it is decentralized. The move away from grand leaders who direct the organization works for SGW and, given the history of Afro-American political struggle, seems an option worthy of consideration. Indeed, the political landscape of Afro-America, dotted with various black elected officials and other luminaries who float above any geographic area—and here I think of Jesse Jackson—demonstrates the utility of the idea of decentralization and not having one leader. One positive aspect of having numerous black women and men working toward black self-determination is that controlling them is more problematic for hostile white organizations and people than would be the case if there were but one leader.

Informed by the insights offered in *The Last Days of Louisiana Red,* the sixties appear as a tragicomedy of intraracial strife and intrigue. Ed Yellings is murdered, his two sons kill each other, and Minnie is shot. In the shadows are the manipulative white man, Maxwell Kasavubu, and his black female accomplice, Nanny Lisa. Both work arduously to destroy SGW and all black expressions of political and spiritual self-determination. These characters appear less fantastic than instructive when we consider the well-structured surveillance and infiltration program of the Federal Bureau of Investigation (Tackwood, Blackstock). Once the FBI located what it considered the eye of the storm—the Black Panthers—it labeled them the most profound threat to national security and then set about murdering them. The FBI hounded most of the activists of the sixties, attempting to lock them up or simply to provoke a situation that would make killing them politically acceptable.

Papa LaBas is no fool and knows these things. The only way for black organizations truly to function is to remove themselves from center stage and quietly go about creating resources that will allow them to achieve their goals.

In the broadest sense, *The Last Days of Louisiana Red* attributes the conflicts and problems of the black community to a lack of literacy, a lack of historical understanding. It suggests that political change for Afro-Americans can come only through the filter of the precedents and lessons of the past. Without these, even individuals who work to improve black life will succeed only in tying soaring black aspirations to the limited options available within the framework of Euro-American thinking.

References

"And Now Yale." *Time,* 4 May 1970, p. 59.

"And Then There Were None." *Time,* 27 April 1970, p. 28.

Baraka, Amiri. "Why I Changed My Ideology." *Black World,* July 1975, pp. 30–42.

————. "The Need For a Cultural Base to Civil Rites & Bpower Movements." In *Raise Race Rays Raze.* New York: Random House, 1971. Pp. 39–48.

"Behind the Turmoil at Yale: Black Power and the Courts." *U.S. News and World Report,* 11 May 1970, pp. 41–42.

Blackstock, Nelson. COINTELPRO: The FBI's Secret War on Political Freedom. New York: Vintage Books, 1975.

Blassingame, John. *The Slave Community: Plantation Life in the Antebellum South.* New York: Oxford University Press, 1972.

"Booklet That Shocked Congress; Black Panther Coloring Book." *U.S. News and World Report,* July 1969, p. 4.

Buckley, W.F., Jr., "Have a Panther to Lunch." *National Review,* 10 February 1970, p. 68.

"Caged Panthers." *Time,* 16 March 1970, p. 57.

Chandler, C. "Black Panther Killings in Chicago." *New Republic,* 10 January 1969, pp. 21–24.

"Close Look at Black Panther Shootouts." *U.S. News and World Report,* 22 December 1969, pp. 25–26.

Cruse, Harold. *The Crisis of the Negro Intellectual.* New York: Morrow, 1967.

Ellul, Jacques. *Propaganda: The Formation of Men's Attitudes.* New York: Vintage Books, 1973.

"Gathering of the Clans; Three-Day Conference in Oakland Summoned and Run by the Black Panthers. *Newsweek,* 4 August 1969, p. 32.

Gayle, Addison, ed. *The Black Aesthetic.* Garden City, N.Y.: Doubleday, 1972.

Genovese, Eugene. *Roll Jordan Roll: The World the Slaves Made.* New York: Pantheon Books, 1974.

"Guns and Butter." *Newsweek,* 5 May 1969, pp. 40–41.

Gwaltney, John, comp. *Drylongso: A Self-Portrait of Black America*. New York: Random House, 1980.

Hare, Nathan. "What Happened to the Black Movement." *Black World*, January 1976, pp. 20–32.

"Heavy Baggage: The Raid on the Panther Headquarters." *Nation*, 20 July 1970, p. 37.

"Is It Too Late for You to Be Pals with a Black Panther?" *Esquire*, November 1970, pp. 141–47.

"Jungle Justice for the Panthers." *America*, 30 May 1970, p. 573.

Karenga, Maulana. "Which Road: Nationalism, Pan-Africanism, Socialism?" *Black Scholar*, October 1974, pp. 21–31.

Levine, Laurence. *Black Culture and Black Consciousness: Afro-American Folk Thought from Slavery to Freedom*. New York: Oxford University Press, 1977.

Lewin, N. "Justice Cops Out: The Chicago Shoot-In; Report of the January 1970 Grand Jury." *New Republic*, 6 June 1970, pp. 14–18.

Madthubuti, Haki. "Enemy from the White Left, White Right and in Between." *Black World*, October 1974, pp. 36–47.

———. "The Latest Purge." *Black Scholar*, September 1974; pp. 43–57.

Marable, Manning. *Blackwater: Historical Studies in Race, Class Consciousness, and Revolution*. Dayton, Ohio: Black Praxis Press, 1981.

"Marked for Extinction." *Nation*, 22 December 1969, p. 684.

"More on Panthers." *Nation*, 29 December 1969, p. 717.

Munford, C. J. "The Fallacy of Lumpen Ideology." *Black Scholar*, July–August 1973, pp. 47–51.

Record, Wilson. "The Development of the Communist Position on the Negro Question in the United States." *Phylon* 19 (1958): 306–26.

Newton, H.P. "Black Panthers." *Ebony*, August 1969, pp. 106–8.

Newton, Huey. *To Die for the People*. New York: Random House, 1972.

"Open Season on Panthers?" *Christian Century*, 24 December 1969, p. 1634.

Palmer, L.F., Jr. "Out to Get the Panthers: FBI and Chicago Police." *Nation*, 28 July 1969, pp. 78–82. "Panther Hunt: Arrests in the Alex Rackly Killing." *Newsweek*, 1 September 1969, pp. 22a–22b. "Persecution and Assassination of the Black Panther Party as Directed by Guess Who." *National Review*, 30 December 1969, pp. 1306–7. "Police and Panthers at War." *Time*, 12 December 1969, p. 20. "Police and Panthers: Growing Paranoia." *Time*, 19 December, 1969, pp. 14–16.

Reed, Ishmael. *Conjure*. Amherst: University of Massachusetts Press, 1970.

———. *The Last Days of Louisiana Red*. New York: Random House, 1974.

Salaam, Kalamu. "Tell No Lies, Claim No Easy Victories." *Black World*, October 1974, pp. 43–57.

Schancke, D.A. "Panthers Against the Wall." *Atlantic*, May 1970, pp. 55–61.

Stern, R. "Fred Hampton's Apartment." *Nation*, 23 March 1970, pp. 325–26.

Tackwood, Louis E. *The Glass House Tapes.* New York: Avon Books, 1973.

"Too Late for the Panthers? Chicago and Los Angeles Confrontations with the Police." *Newsweek,* 22 December 1969, pp. 26–27.

Wallace, Michelle. *Black Macho and the Myth of the Superwoman.* New York: Dial Press, 1979.

Walters, Ronald. "Marxism-Leninism and the Black Revolution." *Black Books Bulletin;* Fall 1975, pp. 12–17.

Conclusion

Regardless of the literary choices the writers whose works are studied here make, all of their characters who manage to learn from and move beyond the constraints and opportunities of the sixties do so because they achieve historical literacy. In discovering themselves in the context of Afro-American history, they become more than themselves. The alienating experience of black soldiers in Vietnam is dashed against the broad rock of historical precedent: they learn that they are not the first generation of black men who fought to protect the rights of foreigners that they themselves did not fully enjoy. The civil rights activists, filled with energy and idealism, believing in the American Dream, are able to move beyond the bitter realization that this country does not always operate with one set of rules not based on color when they seek answers within traditions of the black church. Instead of a slow and steady descent into debilitating hatred and recrimination, they are able to soar because of precedents they discover in the culture. The black power advocates, having seen grand plans for racial solidarity fractured and destroyed by agents from outside and betrayal from within, must defy the odds that logic suggests and find subtle solutions to questions of unity. Usually, the concept of a single head or leader is replaced by the idea of a federated head, all heads under the sway of a shared value system.

The novels in which the characters achieve the highest level of historical understanding are the ones with the most innovative structures—William's *Captain Blackman,* Walker's *Meridian,* and Reed's

189

Last Days of Louisiana Red. These novels are similar in the nonlinear and cyclical way in which they approach time. The retelling of the same story in different settings has a ritualistic dimension that is similar to purging oneself to allow new information to flow in. These novels also incorporate different literary genres. The use of plays, historical documents, and the intermingling of people from the real world with fictional characters all work to make the texts multi-faceted and to undercut traditional boundaries separating fiction and reality. The novelists want us to question comfortable and long-held interpretations of history. More fundamentally, they want us to question the methods we use to arrive at the truth.

The novels in this group are superb examples of one direction that contemporary Afro-American literature has taken. Afro-American novelists are creating worlds in their fiction which suggest links to subtle and intuitive knowledge that Afro-Americans do not often use. Such novelists write from the African and Afro-American experience using systems of thought and feeling from the Afro-American historical reservoir.

The other novels treated here began as personal searches for meaning and direction, but they all conclude with the individual either merging with some tradition in the community or seeing the need to do so. In any case, the message is the same as the one in the more experimental novels: historical understanding, the ability to discover oneself in the context of racial history—what I call literacy—is paramount.

Because of the nature of Afro-American literature, it is not surprising that the novels I have analyzed here should throw light on events in the world. In its most developed state, Afro-American literature embodies an epistemology that is as true as any used by social scientists. Indeed, much of the criticism of this literature suggests its need to relate to external reality (Baker, Stepto). This was certainly my intent in the book.

The meanings of the sixties for Afro-Americans deserve continued and fuller treatment. I have attempted to demonstrate the centrality of contemporary Afro-American literature to discovering some of those meanings.

References

Baker, Houston. *The Journey Back.* Chicago: University of Chicago Press, 1980.

Henderson, Stephen. *Understanding the New Black Poetry.* New York: Morrow, 1973.

Stepto, Robert B. "Teaching Afro-American Literature: Survey or Tradition." In *Afro-American Literature: The Reconsideration of Instruction,* edited by Dexter Fisher and Robert B. Stepto. New York: Modern Language Press, 1978. Pp. 8–24.

Index

149, 156; Defined: 5–6; Freedom and literacy: 5–11, 19, 24, 30, 33, 41, 43, 50–51, 59, 90, 99, 107, 120–21, 130–32, 141, 149, 166, 170; *Last Days of Louisiana Red:* 166, 170; *Look What They Done to My Song:* 120–21, 130–32; *Meridian:* 99, 107; and Self-definition: 40, 190; and Self-determination: 39, 133, 141–42, 156; *Tragic Magic:* 59; and War experience: 18–19

"Racial Crisis: A Consensus" (magazine article), 91

Racism: and Black Power novels: 82, 90–91; and Black women: 94–95, 108; *Captain Blackman:* 28–30, 32–34, 36–38, 40–41; and Civil Rights novels: 82; *Coming Home:* 43, 45–48, 50–53, 56–57; *Cotillion:* 149, 151, 157, 162; and Democratic Party: 88; Easing of tension: 25; Intraracial betrayal: 120, 122–23, 136, 166–67, 170–71, 175, 178; *Last Days of Louisiana Red:* 166, 169, 173–74, 177, 179; *Look What They Done to My Song:* 120–22, 130–31, 133–35; *Meridian:* 102, 109; and Military: 17–24, 28–30, 33–34, 36–38, 40–41, 43, 45–48, 50–53, 56–58, 60–66, 75; and Police: 120–22, 130–31, 133, 135; Propaganda of integration: 20–23, 32–33, 40; *Tragic Magic:* 58, 60–67, 70, 75

Rainbow Coalition (Jesse Jackson), 7
Reagon, Bernice, 137
Reed, Ishmael: 4, 8, 79, 81, 82, 83, 90, 189; Aesthetics: 168–70; *Conjure:* 168, 182; *Mumbo-Jumbo:* 168
Reese, F.D., 102
Religion (*see also* Spirituality; Church): 81, 86, 94, 95; *Cotillion:* 156; *Last Days of Louisiana Red:* 168, 172, 174; *Look What They Done to My Song:* 138; *Meridian:* 108, 110; *Tragic Magic:* 75
"Right to Vote a Must" (magazine article), 85
Robeson, Paul, 146
Roberts, Gene, 69, 70, 127
Rogers, R., 95
Romanticism, 6, 12(n)
Rudwick, Elliot, 84, 89

Salaam, Kalamu, 172
Sanchez, Sonia, 151
Saturation, 5–6
Scatting, 59
Schwerner, Mickey, 73, 87
Seale, Bobby, 9
Self-definition: 4, 11, 18, 79, 89, 93–94, 190; *Captain Blackman:* 28, 32, 38, 40; *Cotillion:*

144, 149, 156, 159; *Look What They Done to My Song:* 123; *Meridian:* 102, 109
Sellers, Cleve, 9, 66, 68, 69, 70, 73, 84, 85, 86, 88, 103, 104, 106, 107, 133
Sergeant Rutledge (movie), 60
Set, 168
Shaffer, George, 20, 21
Sitting Bull, 103
Sixties: 3–4, 6, 9, 11, 79, 90, 93, 189–90; *Captain Blackman:* 28, 37–38; *Cotillion:* 159–60; Defined: 3; *Last Days of Louisiana Red:* 166, 169–70, 173, 175, 177, 179–81, 183–85; *Look What They Done to My Song:* 123, 130–31, 133–34; *Meridian:* 112, 117; *Tragic Magic:* 69, 73
Slavery, 6, 18, 21, 55–56, 89, 123, 133, 136, 153, 163, 173–74, 181–82
Smith, Scott B., 70
Smitherman, Geneva, 4
"SNCC and the Jews" (magazine article), 73
Snead, Gerald, 20–21
Socialization: 30, 133; *Captain Blackman:* 27, 30–31, 35–37; *Coming Home:* 43, 45–57; *Cotillion:* 142, 149, 153, 155, 158, 160–64; *Look What They Done to My Song:* 132; *Meridian:* 98–99, 101–03; and military: 19, 21; *Tragic Magic:* 58, 60, 63, 65
"Soul Alley" (magazine article), 51
Souls of Black Folk (W.E.B. DuBois), 12(n)
Southern Christian Leadership Conference (SCLC), 23, 106, 137
Spirituality (*see also* Church; Religion): 8, 79–81, 96; *Coming Home:* 51; *Cotillion:* 151–52; *Last Days of Louisiana Red:* 166–68, 175, 184–85; *Look What They Done to My Song:* 123–24, 132, 135–38; *Tragic Magic:* 75
Stembridge, Jane, 67–68, 105
Stepto, Robert, 5–6, 8, 12(n), 190
Stereotypes: 17–18, 22, 32, 85; *Captain Blackman:* 17–18, 40; *Coming Home:* 51–53; *Cotillion:* 146, 162; *Last Days of Louisiana Red:* 167–68, 182–84; *Meridian:* 101–02, 112
Strode, Woody, 60
Student, Non-Violent Coordinating Committee (SNCC): 23, 83–89, 92; *Look What They Done to My Song:* 125, 127–31, 136–37; *Meridian:* 102, 105–06; *Tragic Magic:* 66–73
Sweet Honey in the Rock, 137
The System of Dante's Hell (Amiri Baraka), 142

Tackwood, Louis E., 185
Terry, Wallace II, 20–21, 24–25, 28, 31, 37–39